Finding My Voice Through Emotions & Cancer

I Love Pink

PHYLLIS DUNK

I Love Pink
Finding My Voice Through Emotions & Cancer
Copyright © 2020 by Phyllis Dunk

Editorial Note: All rights reserved. Contents may not be reproduced in whole or part without the express written consent of the publisher. No parts of the manual may be reproduced, stored in a retrieval system, or transmitted in any form or by any means—electronically, mechanically, photocopied, recorded, scanned, or other—except for brief quotations in critical reviews or articles, without the prior written permission of the publisher.

Unless otherwise indicated, all scripture quotations, references and definitions are from the Authorized King James Version © 1987; The New King James Version © 1982 by Thomas Nelson, Inc.; The New International Version 1973, 1978, 1984 by International Bible Society by the Zondervan Corporation; The Amplified Bible Old Testament © 1962, 1964, 1965, 1987 by the Zondervan Corporation; The Amplified New Testament © 1954, 1958, 1987 by the Lockman Foundation; The Message. Copyright © 1993, 1994, 1995, 1996, 2000, 2001, 2002.

Phyllis Dunk
dunk@sbcglobal.net
214-326-5033 | www.eaglesiti.org

ISBN # 978-1-949826-20-3

All rights reserved

Published by: EAGLES GLOBAL Publishing | Frisco, Texas
In conjunction with the 2019 Eagles Authors Course
Cover & interior designed by DestinedToPublish.com | (773) 783-2981

Dedication
To My Best Friend

I would like to dedicate this book to my husband, Kennith Ray Dunk. I love this man with all of my heart. He is truly my best friend. He has seen the good, the bad, and the ugly in me and still loved me through it all. He has experienced this journey with me for over twenty-five years and helped me become the woman I am today.

This man let me stand and cry on his shoulders so I could be strengthened and see myself. It takes a special person to be kindhearted during calamity, and this man has taught me to love and to be patient in times of trouble. As a godly man, he loved me when I didn't love myself. Thank you, babe, for being my rock. I'll love you forever. It's been a wonderful life.

I Love Pink

Acknowledgments

To God, who is my ultimate best friend. He has been my strength when I was weak. When I didn't understand myself, he was my peace. His word manifested and gave me life.

To my children, Rae D'Ann, Phyllissa, and Joshua. Thank you for enriching my life. I drew strength from each one of your God-given gifts. I pray that God will increase your gifts to help others. There were times when I needed to laugh, dance, sing, or be overly dramatic, and still be mama. Thank you for listening to my poems and offering feedback. I have watched you grow and mature through this chronicle of work just as I did. For every tear and emotion, I thank you, Rae-ray; I thank you, Essa; I thank you, Josh. I love you!

To my mama, Annie Dobson, who cared for me in her home. She was my personal nurse. She loved me to healing. I love you, Mama, and I will always miss you.

To my stepdad, Adam Dobson, who embodied a quiet strength. I honor you for your love.

To my big sis, Cynthia Williams, who made sure I rested and never overworked myself. She would say, "Girl, you betta lay down and you can't do that." She wanted to make sure I didn't do too much.

To my main oncology doctor, whose name I will never forget because it rhymed with pain: Dr. Fain. He was a patient man. I used to ask him so many silly questions. He made sure I didn't panic and continued to fight. He could look at me and know if I was tired or when I was getting stronger. His care was meticulous.

To the nurses at John Peter Smith who made me to feel some comfort after treatments. The care that they provided me was a blessing. To them, I was a person, not the disease.

To my church family at Destiny Pointe Christian Center. The love that I experienced from this family was instrumental in my maintaining peace. The meals, the childcare, and the genuine love and friendship will always be remembered.

To Pastor Renee Hornbuckle. I have watched this woman of God handle enormous stresses in her personal life as well as in the vast church reorganization. She is the epitome of grace. She taught me to trust God in the process of achieving success. Thank you, Pastor!

To my Dance Tribe. I thank you all. I have learned so much from you: how to show grace and boldness, how to make sacrifices, and how to listen to God's voice. You stood with me through dance and mime when I was weak. I will never move alone. My tribe is always with me. I love you dearly.

Contents

How to Use This Book ix

Introduction xi

SECTION I | *Love*

You, Then Me, Then We 1
Magnet Love 2
My Reflections: Love 3
And You Talked: 2013 7
My Reflections: "And You Talked" 9

SECTION II | *Low Self-Esteem*

My Mirror 13
On That Day 14
He Gave Me Dignity on That Day 15
My Reflections: Low Self-Esteem 17
The Blank Page 22
The Clown in Me 23
I in Me 24
Size 11 25

SECTION III | *Anger & Lying*

Thank You Cancer: 2-22-13 29
My Reflection: Anger 31
A Lie Reality 34
My Reflection: Lies 36

SECTION IV | Humility

The Cross 41
My Reflection: "The Cross" 44
Humble 46
My Reflection: Humility 47

SECTION V | The Drunk, Children & the Addiction

Children Are A Blessing 53
The Actor, the Dancer, & the Singer 55
My Reflection: Children / Addiction 56
Addictions 61

SECTION VI | Worship

A Place 65
Hard Work 66
Wake Up 67
You Are 68
When to Worship 69
I'll Never Leave You 70
Covered From 71
Near the Light 72
My Reflection: Worship 73

SECTION VII | What More Can I Say About My Journey

What More Can I Say About My Journey 81

SECTION VIII | Worry

What If? 91
Woulda, Coulda, Shoulda 92
My Reflections: Woulda, Coulda, Shoulda 94
Say This Prayer 97

SECTION IX | Wonder

Little Flower 101

Cancer 103
Sunflower 104
My Reflections: Wonder 105
The Place 107

SECTION X | *Fear, Joy & Rejection*

False Evidence Appearing Real 111
My Reflections: Fear 112
My Dance 118
My Reflections: Joy / Rejection 120
A Merry Heart 122

SECTION XL | *Death Aging*

A Father's Love 127
My Reflections: A Father's Love 128
A Poem for My Mama 131
My Reflections: A Poem for My Mama 132
Ouch 136
The Other Side of 50 137
My Reflections: Aging 138

SECTION XII | *Boldness*

Be Bold 143
Living Our Dreams 144
My Reflections: Boldness 146
I Have a Wonderful Life 148

Wrap Up 150

I Love Pink

THE DESIGN
HOW TO USE THIS BOOK

I created this book as a written inward journey. I wanted a different kind of book, a book I could read and be creative with. This is not an ordinary poetry book. It requires some action on your part. You'll need a journal, a pen, a pencil, markers, an open mind, and an open spirit to receive from God. The Bible says in Proverbs 8:35, "For whoever finds me finds life and receives favor from the Lord."

For some of you, this may be a quick read. Most of you may find yourselves reading one poem over and over, which should happen. Take your time. If you rush, you may miss what God is saying to you. This is a twenty-five-year emotional investment for me. For seven years, I was just stuck on how to publish and tell my story. Over the last six months, I've had revelations and memories flooding in. So, please, take your time. I ask that you pray that God would speak to you.

If you know me, then you know that this is going to be special. There are empty pages for you to write, create lists, doodle, or draw out your thoughts after you read a poem or two. I tried to date most of the poems to show the timeline. Please have an open mind. After each section, I wrote my reflections about the subjects mentioned in the preceding poems. Those sections contain my personal victories and processes. Reading about my journey may seem awkward at first, but trust that you will find yourself feeling like crying, laughing, and being angry. If you feel these emotions, don't fight them. Try to understand the source and process them. Write down what you feel. Pray and ask God for understanding. There will be this amazing peace that will overtake you as you take this creative journey with me. You have to put in something in order to get something. It really took a whole village to raise me emotionally. Your name may not be in this book, but you are a part of my life. I thank you.

Emotions can be sparked by one word. It's all okay. Sometimes you have to go through a range of emotions to figure yourself out: What triggers me? Why do I react to certain words that are spoken? Why am I fearful or angry? We all have emotions. Most of them, we just don't understand. Please use this as a simple tool to better yourself emotionally. There are plenty of books on the market that will outline the hows or dos and don'ts. I make no claim that this book will heal emotions. This is my personal emotional journey, my story about how I found my voice. I will claim that this is a good starting point. (If you need further help after reading this book, I recommend you contact a spiritual counselor or a psychologist to assist you in going even deeper.)

Lose yourself, and then you will find yourself. In Matthew 10:39 it says, "Whoever finds his life will lose it and whoever loses his life for my sake will find it."

In this book, there are poems that are required to be read over and over. My style is very different and sometimes abstract. Sometimes I had no idea what I was writing until I was nearly finished. I cried a lot during the process of writing and rewriting. I felt like I had given birth. This was a big baby. I may use rhyme at times, but then sometimes I don't. Some of my pieces have rhythms, some don't. Once again: lose yourself and then find yourself.

If you are ready to journey with me . . .

Just pray & continue reading.

Introduction

Over twenty-five years ago, I was encouraged to start writing my thoughts down through journaling. This was to be a selfish journey. I do not consider myself a writer or an expert. I learned that if you really apply the word of God, be willing to do the basic work, and keep a sense of humor, change will occur in your life. Your spiritual and emotional state will be healthier.

About seven years ago, I started thinking about what I should do with all these poems, thoughts, and emotions. I began to write down more of my thoughts, and then my thoughts turned into more poems. I heard a voice deep within me say, "Write a book." I thought, sure, but I don't have enough to fill a book. I need to write some more poems.

I asked God to help. We must be careful what we ask God for. He heard me. This request caused a ripple of experiences, intense emotions, and memories. I would write at different periods of my life. Writing became a little obsession at times. I had to do it. I began to chronicle my emotional life. Then there were periods of no writing. I had no idea how deep I was about to go. I have rewritten this book over and over, and I have discovered I went through a lot during the cancer years and beyond. My journey began with writing about the pressures of life, low self-esteem, cancer, and worshipping God—all great topics, right? It was in those poems that I poured out my heart.

Then, on January 17, 2013, I had an encounter with Prophetess Mwaka. I went to the altar for prayer. She said that she saw a book when she touched my hands, and she saw even more books, and more books, and more books. I was so amazed that God spoke to me through her. I just stood there, pondering. I didn't shout, roll around on the floor, or speak in tongues. I knew it was God speaking. I wanted to hear clearly, without any emotionalism. Something changed inside of me. I have never been the same since that day. She gave me the hard push in the spirit and the confirmation I needed to complete this task. Weeks before this powerful encounter, I had already begun to organize the contents of a book. I numbered my poems and wrote little commentaries about some of them.

I talked to my pastor after this event. I wanted to know what steps I needed to take in presenting a "finished product." Since she had written a bestseller, I thought she would know best what steps were needed next. She felt that I should complete the task and recommended that I submit a copy to her to read. I knew I was on track with organizing and designing my book. A few days before I talked to her, I had set a timeline. I wanted to make sure I maintained certain goal dates. I projected April 2013 as the month I wanted to submit the book to publishers. I was still not ready. I realized that I had years of emotions buried deep within me that needed to be dealt with. My spiritual and emotional growth had been hindered. I had to go back and go deeper many times, back to my cancer years to understand who I am now, who I was then, and who I need to be. Am I just an "angry black woman"? Am I still a sad and disappointed woman? Do I still wear a mask that I don't know I have on? Am I fake? Does low self-esteem still have a grip on me that I cannot shake? Have I overcome rejection and fear? Am I still numb to life? I needed to answer all these questions. I had to go back and go deeper. I was now ready to face myself.

During the cancer years, what I looked like on the outside made me very uncomfortable. I lost my hair, I lost a little weight, and I looked tired in my face. I had on a mask of sickness. What I was feeling on the inside somewhat frightened me; I was fighting negative thoughts constantly. Who was I? Why was I always comparing myself to others? How could I be angry and sin not? There were times when I was so happy when I should have been sad. There were times when I was quiet when I shouldn't have been. Why wouldn't I speak up? How could I process these emotions? I wanted to free myself of all the junk I had stored up inside of me. I took simple tools and began to write, draw, and doodle. I am a creative person. I clowned, mimed, danced, created props, and designed sets for our plays at church. I needed a creative outlet. I began to think about all the stuff I had been going through, but was too afraid to admit. I realized I was stuck.

I not only had cancer once, but twice. I was diagnosed with breast cancer in 1994 and I went through chemo and radiation treatments for months. The doctor tried to tell me gently. He held my hand and said, "If it looks like a duck and quacks like a duck, it's a duck. You have cancer." I thought, what an unusual way to convey terrible news. Then I realized God still had a sense of humor and that joke was just for me. I was shocked, but I had no emotions. I had cried enough already. The doctor waited for me to be more emotional. I wanted to be in control. I was numb and in shock. Looking back, I probably should have cried. I asked the doctor, "What is our plan of action?" Faith was present. He said total mastectomy, chemo, and radiation.

December of 1994, I had the operation. My mom's face was the first face I saw when I awakened. She just smiled. In 1995, I started treatments. It was a rough year. My emotions were all over the place. I cried by myself and slept a lot. Every three weeks I would get an infusion of this red drug. It looked like blood. It's known as the "red devil" (Doxorubicin, common name Adriamycin). They used to deliver it with a little paper bag to conceal the color. The infusions would take two to three hours, a very slow drip trip. Imagine watching this red fluid for two hours: drip . . . drip . . . drip. After the treatments, I lived in slow motion, walked in slow motion, even talked slowly. I remember using a towel to wipe my mouth because I was drooling involuntarily. I had no control, was not able to verbally pray. I couldn't hold a thought. All I would say was "Jesus!"

After two months, losing my hair was very emotional. I was so low emotionally and was dealing with low self-esteem. Depression was my friend. Loss of appetite. I was hungry, but couldn't eat much or ate nothing at all. Throwing up was one adverse reaction from the drugs that I hated. Sometimes I threw up nothing. The pain from this was very intense and violent. I would shake and just kneel in front of the toilet.

I remember cooking a wonderful meal and just sitting at the table, looking at everyone eat. I cooked turkey spaghetti with chunky veggies, one of my favorites. I prepared a nice, green leafy salad, ranch dressing, sweet cornbread, and sweet iced tea with lemon. I don't remember what we had for dessert. It could have been cheesecake, another family favorite. The acidity from the tomato sauce burned my mouth. I took one bite and was in so much pain. I just sat there for a while, then served my family that night because I just couldn't eat. I didn't want to ruin our mealtime with my ailments.

Going grocery shopping was done in slow motion. I just held on to the basket because I couldn't think or compare food items. I got confused and lost focus. I used to love comparing and selecting the best for my family. It was too much for me. My mind couldn't process fast enough. My husband would ask me a question about which item we used. I just shrugged my shoulders to gesture, "I don't know." He knew then that he would have to take the lead and finish shopping. I remember going to a clothing store because my husband felt like I needed to buy myself something to wear. I came out with this yellow fleece warmup. I wasn't socializing so I was thinking, I'm only hanging around the house, so I'll just buy a warmup. He said, "Is that all you bought?"

I slept a lot. I think I was in fear of throwing up. All of the extra movement would cause an episode. I remember getting stronger. The treatments began to kill those pesky cancer cells and I was beginning to live, move, and think. My last chemo treatment was a day of celebration! I cried and ate good.

In 1999. I was diagnosed again, with colon cancer, but God! I didn't have to go through any chemo and radiation treatments. I remember having an eagerness to have a bowel movement, sitting down, and then getting up, looking in the toilet, and seeing blood. At first I wanted to panic, but I heard a small voice say, "Stop looking at the blood. You are covered by the blood." There was a peace that came over me that I cannot explain. I knew this was God's will for me and everything was going to be all right again.

They did remove five inches of my colon, my gallbladder, and my ovaries. I found that out after they had gone in. I guess it was a little exploratory surgery. The doctors knew that what they found needed to be removed. After the surgeries, the pathologist said it was all removed—no cancer cells and no chemo. Glory to God!

The recovery was very painful. I'd had three surgeries in one. A section of my colon was removed, then sewn back together; my ovaries were removed; and my gallbladder. That was a lot of trauma to the body. I walked around the hospital with a pillow in front of my stomach to bear the pain. Why do they make you walk so much? I guess to help your body heal and make sure every organ gets back into place.

My kids were not happy to see me in the hospital. They looked so sad. Laughter became one of my medicines. The joy of the lord was my strength. I had a merry heart. I would tell myself, "God got this; I don't." When I had dark days, I looked for the light and found God. I found myself just happy to be alive. The wife and mother returned. I almost overdosed on joy. I laughed a lot and became "Bubbles the Clown" without makeup. I knew that the present suffering cannot be compared to the glory that was going to be revealed in my life later. Glory! This is the later!

All of that was still just a fraction of what I was dealing with. Why would God allow this to happen to *me*? I was a good person. I never hurt anyone. I had something to say, but I didn't know how. All my life, I knew there was something special about me. I was different. I had friends, but it seemed I would always put up this wall. Now, I realized that I was not alone. I have encountered people during my treatments who are just like me: searching for themselves. Words have the power to heal or destroy. In James 3:10 (NIV), it says "Out of the same mouth come praise and cursing. My brothers and sisters, this should not be." I was afraid to speak in fear of being rejected. I wasn't in fear about speaking anything negative. I was in fear of not knowing how to handle confrontation once I spoke. Fear can cause you to be stuck. Who told me to be quiet? I did. Who told me that I had no voice? I did.

The word of God says that my tongue is the pen of a skillful writer. I decided to embark on this long road and let life happen *for* me and not *to* me. No more the victim, but a conqueror! I have the assurance that God allowed things to happen for my good. All that I went through did not feel good, but it was for my good. Chronicling and then exposing my life, thoughts, and emotions is a brave thing to do. What will people think? I was on the surface seven years ago but now I've gone deeper, behind the words I wrote, to uncover life lessons. This was my personal path, not anyone else's. The Bible tells us to take every thought captive. What if you need to get to the core of a thought (the why) or emotion in order to diminish it or understand it? That's what I did.

I can say that, today, I love the woman that I am and that I'm becoming. Perfect? Nope, far from that. I'm still a work in progress. I have learned not to allow emotions to overtake who I am, but simply to understand and manage them. If I'm angry now, I know why. Sometimes it can be petty, but it's what I feel. I've realized that I have the power to manifest and become what I think and speak. I have been driven to complete this book. My life's mantra is "a merry heart doeth good like a medicine" (Proverbs 17:22). I've discovered that I can be happy in the midst of emotions. Laughter is the best medicine I can give to myself. When dealing with my emotions, I've learned to

- Acknowledge my emotions.
- Process and understand why they're present.
- Diminish any long-lasting effects I allow emotions to have using the word of God.
- Spend quality time with God.

I Love Pink

I'm far from being crazy, just different. It just takes work. I have to process how I feel and be real with myself, my true self. I wanted to do better handling my emotions. This was my *why* for writing this book. Thank you for taking this journey with me. I hope you find it fun and revealing.

I Love Pink

SECTION I

Love

I Love Pink

You, Then Me, Then We
7-7-08

One night you beheld me in all of my glory
Only for your eyes to see
You know my story
You, then me, then we
Hand in hand, Heart to heart
forever you will be mine.
We will never part
Forever joined
You, then me, then we.
Like drums we, beat, beat, beat
Passions flowing, love's heat
Boom, boom, one, two
Boom, boom, one, two
You, then me, then we.
The earth has trembled and the sea roared
because we embraced the promise
Love never fails
You, then me, then we.
Our children children's will pick up our rhythm
They will be the promise forever manifested
You, then me, then we.

Magnet Love
7-2-09

The smell of your skin
The light in your eye
The way you walk
The way you talk
When you smile, my heart melts.
If love was like a magnet, then I would place myself next to you
until you end and I end and we begin.
In the beginning, our love will rule
In the beginning, there's no end
You see, it's always
in the beginning
our love was new, fresh, and alive
and felt like butterflies
We declared Our Love
Will be irremovable, unified, incorporated,
joined, integrated, fused, and
Undefiled.
When two become one,
nothing can separate us.
What storms shall we endure as one?
No fire is too hot. We've felt them all.
Rain may come, only to recede.
For this weight is a blessing and not a curse.
We have magnet love.

My Reflections
Love

∽

"Love is patient, love is kind. It does not envy, it does not boast, it is not proud. It does not dishonor others, it is not self-seeking, it is not easily angered, it keeps no record of wrongs. Love does not delight in evil but rejoices with the truth. It always protects, always trusts, always hopes, always, perseveres. Love never fails" (1 Corinthians 13:4–8).

If I could live by this scripture all the time, my life would be great! I know life presents issues that seem to dilute the word of God and make it ineffective. When I realized I needed to activate the word of God for my marriage in this area, I was empowered. My faith was restored. How could I have been so selfish?

First Peter told me that I needed to submit myself to my husband and win him over with a quiet and gentle spirit from the inside. It didn't matter that I was weak physically or what I looked like on the outside. My husband was to treat me with respect so his prayers would not be hindered. I used to wear him out with that scripture. All he could say was "you're right." I was wrong-right. The word of God is supposed to be used to free people, not to judge them or hold them captive—wrong-right.

"Wives, in the same way submit yourselves to your own husbands so that, if any of them do not believe the word, they may be won over without words by the behavior of their wives, when they see the purity and reverence of your lives. Your beauty should not come from outward adornment, such as elaborate hairstyles and the wearing of gold jewelry or fine clothes. Rather, it should be that of your inner self, the unfading beauty of a gentle and quiet spirit, which is of great worth in God's sight. For this is the way the holy women of the past who put their hope in God used to adorn themselves. They submitted themselves to their own husbands, like Sarah, who obeyed Abraham and called him her lord. You are her daughters if you do what is right and do not give way to fear.

"Husbands, in the same way be considerate as you live with your wives, and treat them with respect as the weaker partner and as heirs with you of the gracious gift of life, so that nothing will hinder your prayers" (1 Peter 3).

Love is important to everyone. We all want to give love and to be loved. It's part of our human need. You must love yourself before you can love anyone else for real. I had to learn this during the cancer years. This subject can be a little sensitive. I feel it's important as a married woman going through cancer to discuss.

Let me just put the record straight and be real: We love each other very much, but during this particular time in my journey, lovemaking was somewhat put on hold until I could get my body and mind unified and headed toward healing. I didn't want anything to do with it. It took great energy, and I didn't have any. All of my energy was focused on me. I began to realize how selfish I had become. My needs were being met, but not my husband's. How could we have magnet love and "you, then me, then we" if I withheld my body from him? Did I want him to end up in the arms of another woman? I was so wrong.

When I met my husband, he was a talker and a thinker. I loved that about him. We talked about everything. He never pressured me about sex. On our first date, he invited me over to go swimming. I accepted because I was fresh out of a swimming class. I think he was showing off, because he was swimming on the bottom of the pool like a whale.

We were great friends who just loved hanging out. We dated. We went to movies, restaurants, concerts, sporting events, and so on. It all changed one night when we kissed. I felt something in my heart I'd never felt before. He felt it too, but we still hung out as friends.

After two years, I asked him to marry me. He said, "Nah, not for about five years." Well, about three years later, he kinda asked me to marry him at the jacuzzi. I had turned my back to cool off a bit, and when I turned around, he had placed a black box on the side of the tub.

    I asked him, "What is this?"

    He said, "You tell me."

I opened the box and there was a diamond ring inside. My heart just dropped. I was so excited. I asked, "Are you asking me to marry you?"

He said yes. That was an unusual proposal. We were married in 1986. Well, fast-forward, we had three children, and then I was diagnosed with cancer and forgot all about passion. His attempts to rekindle that passion were dismissed by my bouts of throwing up and sleeping all day. My desire to be intimate was nonexistent. Every time I was touched, it felt harsh. I couldn't understand why. Maybe I was feeling like less than a woman because of the drugs and loss of a breast. I can't explain it, but it was very real to me. I did not want to make love or have sex.

My husband has always been gentle with me. After months of this platonic relationship, I prayed to God that my passion and desire would be restored. It came back a little at a time. My husband was grateful for those moments during the cancer years. He was fulfilled! I was his lover and wife again. He could roar like a lion and whisper my name in my ear. He was the king! He was so patient and gentle, and I was the greatest actress in the world. I should have won an Oscar (as a co-star)! I was only acting for a limited time, until I got physically and mentally stronger. Then I roared and whispered his name in his ear and kissed his eyes. "You then, me then we."

Today there's no need to act or pretend. God has given us a freshness. We are still in love after thirty-three years and enjoy holding hands, listening to jazz, and watching sunsets, ocean waves, and each other, sometimes not in that order.

And You Talked
2013

With one hard pop on your butt, it started. Oh, it was a cry at first, but then words formed . . . and you talked.

As a child, you had the ability to talk yourself out of all kinds of trouble. Your mother too young to mother, so God placed another mother queen in your life to nurture your gift with loving kindness. Your mother became your mother/sister . . . and she talked.

In order to cope, you talked to yourself, only to realize that you were born into a rich heritage of talkers, pastors, preachers, bishops, and "Unc," a man who loved you like a son even though he was your great-uncle. . . and he talked.

You were simply rehearsing your destiny. Even in your abyss of darkness, like the prodigal, you emerged determined and triumphant . . . and you talked! Your line brothers knew of your gift. You talked to them above the college pledging rhetoric.

When you met me, the love of your life . . . you talked. You had me so mesmerized that I really thought 777-9311 was your phone number. You realized that talking was a gift.

You never meet a stranger. Always talking . . . talking. You are an amazing person. How can someone spend two hours in church with people and then, right after services, speak to these same people in the parking lot, from the car, blowing the horn and waving goodbye as if you just saw them for the first time? And as strange as that sounds, how about these same people reacting the same way, smiling and waving? Who does that? That's a sign of a gift, and I know signs. I'm prophetic!!!

Your children recognize this gift of encouragement. You speak and they listen, even when you think they are not. One problem they have with you is that they do not understand how you can esteem others above yourself. In time, they will understand. You want people to feel valued.

As your wife, I want to say that you are a warm and wonderful husband. I appreciate all the little things you do for me. I love to be placed in time-out with a candlelit bubble bath. No man has ever touched me the way you do. When I was sick from cancer treatments, you spoke life into me. Your hands—OMG!—are instruments of healing. You know this body very well. You know how to crack my back with one big hug and burp me like a baby. You know the good, the bad, and the ugly in me, and you've loved me through it all.

So, on this day, we celebrate you!!! Yes, you and your gifts of wisdom, kindness, patience, love, friendship, and encouragement will not go unnoticed. You have impacted our lives. We just want to say and show you how much we love you. That's why we have gathered tonight.

Happy birthday to a devoted friend, husband, and father.

We are all better for having you to talk to.

My Reflections
"And You Talked"

"And You Talked" was written for my husband for his sixtieth birthday celebration seven years ago, months in advance. He has inspired me to be a better person. When I wanted to quit, he told me that cancer would not defeat me or kill me. He spoke in faith. I have experienced this man's love and tenderness, and it's unbelievable. He allows me to be me. When Jezebel needed correction, he would definitely speak to her. He is the father I wish I had. He loves so deeply. He would walk a mile to the store just for a few groceries. It is an honor to journey through life with him. He is my best friend and my soul mate.

On our travels, we are such tourists. He lets me plan our excursions, but always finds time to be alone. On our last trip, to Hawaii, he left to go walking early in the morning with swim shoes on. When he returned two hours later, his toes had busted out of them. I spent twenty minutes laughing. We have spent special, moments just sitting and holding hands. We even hold hands while driving sometimes. Really. Yes, really! He loves to talk. I try to listen most of the time.

He's my "baby daddy." He loves his children and wants the best for them. His children called him blessed. They listen to the wisdom that he shares. He is the real-deal dad. He has seen the worst in me and still loves me. ***Agape*** love is demonstrated each and every day through this man. Did I mention he loves to talk? The world is a better place because Mr. Kenneth Dunk was born. I love me some Dunk. I wanted to honor him with this special poem.

Happy Birthday, Baby.

The Blank Page

"Love is . . ." — I Corinthians 13

What comes to mind when you think about love? The sound of water waves moving inshore and out . . . always there.

_____

_____

_____

_____

_____

_____

_____

_____

_____

_____

_____

_____

_____

_____

SECTION II

Low Self-Esteem

My Mirror
12-29-05

When I look into my mirror **lately,**
I see an awesome woman.
My large arms have hugged and nurtured so many.
My broad shoulders have helped to bear the weight
of others' pain when they were weak.
My large, brown eyes can look into the soul of a person
and see all the hurt
and with that same look can heal.
My large mouth has the ability to speak life,
whether it's loud or soft-spoken.
I'm strong and gentle in spirit
and I have been equipped
to give the love that's needed.
God says I'm "more than."
So when I really look into my mirror
I see who God sees
The real me!

On That Day

On that day, all I could say was "Oh, no"
On that day, what I lost, I gained
On that day, my husband gave me dignity
On that day, I did not accept insanity
On that day, God reigned in me
On that day, God revealed himself through a man.
On that day, I learned to love myself
On that day, I was served
On that day, I saw love in someone else's eyes
On that day, I became beautiful again.

He Gave Me Dignity on That Day
7-24-09

This would be the day
The day I realized that as I held on to my hair
I was holding on to the past
The past that told me that I didn't measure up
The past that held my identity
in a negative image full of low self-esteem.
No more rolled-up bandanas to hold it down
It was time to grow up. Time to fly!
My husband gave me dignity on that day.
The ability to finally accept
The loss of my hair.
My glory, My worth
was what was on my head
and not what was in my head.
The third chemo treatment was the moment for me.
Would I dare to peel back layers of hair?
I began with removing the bandana
and then
The hair that was simply lying on my head.
This was no joke, not a time to be funny.
My husband said, "It's time for a trim."
He knew the lie I was living and that I had been tripping.
He knew I needed help.
(For a black woman, having hair is a big deal.)
For a woman, hair is very important
We love hair! We weave it, we lace it, we sew it in,
and at the level I was,
I grew mine! To my shoulders!
This was no time to be silly

I Love Pink

He sat me down in front of a mirror
and gave me dignity.
It was a supernatural thing.
He cut, trimmed and talked.
In my mind he had cut layers of hair
But in reality it was only peach fuzz.
It was to take a few minutes
But you see
When you're building someone up from nothing
minutes turn into hours.
There were layers of fears and
Tears he had to walk me through.
I told him that one day I would be beautiful again
He gave me dignity with love.
He looked me in my eyes through the mirror
And said that I was still beautiful.
When he had finished cutting, trimming, and talking,
I fully accepted the loss of my hair and I was ready To live in the
beauty I was born with from the inside.
Fearfully and wonderfully made.

He gave me dignity on that day.

MY REFLECTIONS
Low Self-Esteem

"On That Day" and "He Gave Me Dignity on That Day" were written on two different levels. "On That Day" was just a quick jot. What was I talking about? I remained on the surface of what I had been through. Losing my hair was a big deal, but I didn't want people to know. "He Gave Me Dignity on That Day" was a deeper revelation of what I was going through.

Low self-esteem had a grip on me, and I had to deal with this oppression I was allowing. Losing my hair was the best thing to happen to me and for me. I had lost myself to my hair. My identity was tied up in my hair. If my hair looked good, then I was good. I loved my hair. My image and my self-esteem were in my hair.

But was my worth in the strands of my hair? Did my long hair make me beautiful? The way I viewed myself from the outside was warped. The reality was that I thought I was ugly to look at. I didn't love myself. My hair was pretty; I wasn't. I was fat and needed to lose weight and I wore a size 11 shoe . . . blah, blah, blah . . . a story I kept on repeat. Was I still beautiful from the inside? How had I become so superficial?

Once again, this illustrated how God used my husband to pull me out through my hair. I will never forget how he treated me. I was watching TV with the kids, and my husband, I think, was actually cutting his hair, prepping for Sunday service. I had made up my mind it was time to remove this facade of hair. I was finally ready to reveal my truth.

I used to wear a bandana on my head to keep the hair in place. My hair sat on my head like a wig. My head had started to itch and smell, and I really needed to wash what little hair remained. I had completed, I think, about three cycles of chemo. I had lost my eyebrows, the hair in my nose. There was no hair on my body anywhere. It had shrank under the strong drugs. The drugs killed any rapidly producing cells, such as hair follicles. My hair was shedding, and it was time for me to come out of denial. I could no longer hide. I would scratch my head and hair would fall out. Who was I fooling? Myself.

I started to remove the hair physically with great ease because it was just standing on my head. After I finished, I went into the restroom and asked my husband to cut it.

He looked at me with so much love and said, "Okay, it's time for a trim. Let me get a chair."

I don't remember if I cried, but I had tears in my eyes. I only had peach fuzz on my head. I was loved and adored as the perceived layers of hair fell to the floor. In my mind it was hair, but in reality it was just a handful. He took time to look at me. He had me to turn my head left and right, tilt up and tilt down. I was put at ease. I accepted it and was relieved to finally take off this mask I was hiding behind, the lie I was telling myself.

Was I emotional? Yes. Was I afraid? Yes. I had to deal with the reality of the moment: I no longer had a beautiful head full of hair. What I also realized was that I simply hated myself and I didn't know who I was. When the hair was gone, I had to deal with the real me and the real truth. Who was I? How could I love myself? Losing my hair was very traumatic. I had to adjust emotionally and physically.

Physically, well, I didn't have to buy any shampoo or conditioner for a while, or any other hair care products. I got my first wig from the American Cancer Society. It was a brown, synthetic hot mess. I couldn't afford to purchase one. A few months later, I was approached by a dear sister, Angela Pitcher. She said she wanted me to get an updated wig. She handed me some money and told me to go get a better one. She'd noticed that the one I had been wearing was so old and worn. It had been exposed to the heat of the oven and the heat of the sun. It was hideous. I was so appreciative. She's a very caring person. By buying a wig for me, she brought my self-esteem up to a whole new level. God had touched her heart. She will always have a special place in my heart.

Since then I've had many hair transformations. When my hair grew out, I had a short little afro. As it grew, I used to wear it permed and wrapped it every night. After a few years, I cut it short again and started double-twisting. For six years now, I've been wearing braids or dreads. My hair has grown considerably. It's really strange that every time I think I want to cut my hair or change the style, someone always compliments me on my dreads and I delay my change.

But it's coming. Change is coming.

In Psalm 139:14 it says, "I praise you because I am fearfully and wonderfully made; your works are wonderful, I know that full well."

I had to live this scripture on a daily basis. When I first started quoting this, I didn't believe it. How was it possible to be beautiful (fearfully and wonderfully made) when I had no hair? It was possible with God. So as a man thinketh, so is he (Proverbs 23:7). I began to quote and believe. I spent a lot of time looking at myself in the mirror. I took my clothes off and looked. I was shocked at first. I was a bald-headed, scared, sick-looking black woman. I have scars that I will have to look at for the rest of my life. There's no covering them up. I have a dark brown square on my chest in the area where my left breast was. During radiation treatments, that area got infected, and I had to use an ointment to minimize the pain. I was so tired during those days. I have a spotted area on my collarbone. I was told that area was treated for lymph nodes. The area where the port-a-catheter was right above my right breast left a three-inch deep scar. I have toenail fungus that I've been treating for years. Physically I will never be 100 percent. Some days I walk and little slower. Bones may crack, but most days my energy level runs on the joy of the Lord and vitamins.

The story of the removal of the port-a-cath was one of incredible endurance on my part. The lead surgeon was out and I had a nervous intern. I was told that this procedure was typical and I didn't need to be fully sedated. I was given a local. Well, this procedure was horrific. The young doctor underestimated the amount of scar tissue that needed to be removed and the amount of local sedation I needed. My body had become one with the port-a-cath and grown around it. Layers had to be cut out. This thing was surrounded by scar tissue. The intern was so frustrated, and I was in so much pain. I still had joy, but I really wanted all this to stop. The look on the doctor's face was that of desperation. He left the room at one point to contact the lead doctor, but he was unavailable. He apologized for causing me so much pain. I had to bear this pain until the tissue was completely removed. The pain I kept comparing it to was childbirth. When the mechanism was finally removed, it looked smaller than I remembered. It had been in my body for close to a year.

I will never forget how I felt imperfect and didn't like myself. I'm sure my behavior showed. The more I quoted Psalm 139:14, the more I began to accept my imperfections as unique personal traits. God had a way of using people to validate my self-esteem. I remember a time after one of the women's fellowships when I was asked to show my scar. I thought nothing about exposing myself. I took it as a unique learning experience for the woman who asked. We went into the bathroom, I lifted up my bra, and there it was: the big brown square void of a breast on my chest. Her look was quite interesting. She was just amazed. I was, too, at the thought that she wanted to see it. She called me brave, another moment designed by God to teach me to accept my scars. Only he could set up that moment to take what is ugly and create something great for someone else. I can look at my scars as battle scars of victories I won. I became beautiful from the inside out.

God used people to help build my broken self-esteem. I was afraid of who I was and what I looked like. To God, it only mattered what was on the inside. Don't be afraid of who you are in a dark season. You can change, just as the seasons change. Winter turns into spring, spring turns into summer, then summer turns into fall. This happens about every three months, but in Texas, it can happen in one day. We have to be comfortable with being uncomfortable.

The Blank Page

"I praise you because I am fearfully and wonderfully made; your works are wonderful, I know that full well." —Psalm 139:14

Have you ever dealt with low self-esteem?

_____

_____

_____

_____

_____

_____

_____

_____

_____

_____

_____

_____

_____

_____

The Clown in Me
3-5-13

The clown in me wants to come out
It's time for the show, but where are the people?
The clown only wanted to play
when no one was around
To jump, laugh, and be silly
To laugh with and not at
Performing a fun trick and laughing loud
Sweating, makeup would drip and run off the face
No one would be afraid.
The clown in me loves to have a good time
Start the music and watch me move
Turn it up and watch me groove
Someone sang "Send in the Clowns"
How can you send a clown that is trapped inside?
The clown in me loves people and
the clown in me loves to be alone.
Happiness has a cost to pay for the clown in me
Smiling on the outside and dead on the inside
God had to reach deep into the clown from the inside
The selfish heart had to be healed
The wounded person needed love
The gift revealed for the world to see
That what was on the outside
was truly on the inside.
Beyond the makeup and the costumes,
The clown was finally free.

I Love Pink

Replace *the clown* in "The Clown in Me" with *I*.
This is how the poem will read:

I in Me
3-12-13

I want to come out
It's time for the show, but where are the people?
I only wanted to play
when no one was around
To jump, laugh and be silly
To laugh with and not at
Performing a fun trick and laughing loud.
Sweating, makeup would drip and run off the face
No one would be afraid.
I love to have a good time
start the music and watch me move
Turn it up and watch me groove
Someone sang "Send in I."
How can you send the I that is trapped inside?
I love people
and I love to be alone.
Happiness has a cost to pay for I
Smiling on the outside and dead on the inside
God had to reach deep into I from the inside
The selfish heart had to be healed
The wounded person needed love
The gift revealed for the world to see
That what was on the outside
was truly on the inside.
Beyond the makeup and the costumes,
I was finally free

Size 11

My shoe size is just right for me
Double ones! I love shoes
What does size matter
when you're walking through mud?
We should be looking up, not down.
I love shoes
My size 11 experiences are just right for me.
God said, "I will put no more on you
than you can bear."
I'm glad that when I wore a size 8
I did not have to bear size 11 issues.
I was young and played with dolls.
If my ideal size was a 7
Could I find more selections?
What does size matter
when you're walking through mud?
We should be looking up, not down.
We all have issues that bring us pain
It's all about how we walk through them.
So I embrace my size 11 hard-to-find shoes because
God knows what size is best for me.
Every time I get a new pair of size 11 shoes,
there's a little discomfort
because I have to break them in.
I know that
with each step, the discomfort becomes
less and less.

Dang! I love shoes!

THE BLANK PAGE

"A merry heart doeth good like a medicine." —Proverbs 17:22

What's in your heart?

SECTION III

Anger & Lying

Thank You Cancer
2-22-13

I want to thank you, Cancer, for invading my body with your death presence. Yes, I thank *you* for the fear of dying that gripped my thoughts for months. This fear told me I was going to die, but instead I became stronger and stronger until I began to hear myself say, "**Live!!!**"

Cancer, you thought you had me when my cousin Sarah (Say-rah) died. Simply it was her time, not mine. That experience made me more determined to *survive*.

Thank you, Cancer, for the numerous chemo and radiation treatments I endured to defeat you! You see, because of you, during those treatments, I came into contact with *so* many great people. I was able to touch people in a profound way. I couldn't have accomplished that without you. These great people helped to restore my health . . . awesome nurses who administered powerful red medication to destroy your tiny cells. Wonderful doctors who had never seen anyone like me go through those annoying little illnesses with such a positive attitude.

Thank you for your symptoms of healing, like frequent bouts of fever, lack of appetite, lack of energy. Oh, Cancer, when I lost my hair, I realized that it mattered more to me what was *on* my head than what was *in* my head. The number one symptom, *throwing up*, was just a way for me to purge myself of all of *your* negative junk.

Thank you because I became closer to my creator, God. I got to the core of who I am. Through the chemo treatments, I learned about nutrition; through radiation, I learned to be at rest and to stop the worrying.

I Love Pink

I thank you for helping me find my purpose. I am an encourager. I learned creative ways of expression: through mime, I learned to worship; through clowning, I'm able to channel all of my joy and zeal for life; and through writing poetry, I can release emotions. Without you, Cancer, I wouldn't have ever gone this deep within myself to pull myself out. What a marvelous gift you have been.

Cancer, I was *so angry* with you when I first met you, but now you're a constant reminder of how much I have grown. You have become my greatest trophy. So now I have a fuller, more rewarding life.

> I'm not just surviving. I'm living.
> I'm living! THANK YOU, CANCER!

My Reflection
Anger

When I was diagnosed with cancer, sure, I was angry. Why me? No! What the heck is this? Look here, God, this is just not right! Why do I have cancer? The fact was, I had cancer, and I had to embrace that reality. The blessing came after I processed and progressed through treatments and reliance on God: I became grateful for cancer. I'd always heard cancer was terrible. Until you've walked in my shoes and lived my life, don't judge my cancer gratefulness.

Thanking cancer, to me, meant thanking the disease for killing the old person I used to be. I realized that having cancer brought me to another level of self that taught me who I was. Some lessons were so deep, I have never been able to express them until now. There was no way I could have thanked cancer during the early recovery stages. I was still physically weak and my faith was immature. One of my struggles was low self-esteem, which I tried to hide. I wrote about the power of low-self-esteem in the previous section. I struggled with who I really was. Losing my hair stripped me of who I thought I was. I was not just a pretty face with beautiful hair. It was more to me than that. God placed gifts in me that helped me heal. This anger, I do believe, was misplaced in the form of low self-esteem: "I have cancer and I don't like the way I look." And I became a mad, angry black woman with a fake mask on: "Now, leave me alone!"

I learned that I needed to break free of these fatal emotions. They were hindering my healing both naturally and spiritually. I was quoting scriptures, then thinking negatively about myself. That was very dangerous. What you think has an impact on what you do. I never used my illness to manipulate anyone emotionally. I tried to present my best self in the midst of pain and uncertainty. I think that's how I became fake.

During my healing, my gifts got stirred up. I became more creative. I have this innate need to create, and it's one of my lifelong therapies. When I first started chemo treatments, I used to collect coupons and organize them. I rarely used them. It was the process my mind needed at the time. I was exercising my mind. I love to use simple items to create, like making hoop earrings unique by wrapping colored pipe cleaners around them or blinging out a picture frame. I blinged out something almost every week.

When I was assigned to be the props master at my church, I was very disappointed. I wanted to act! Those feelings of rejection were coming forth again. Why was I overlooked? God knew what I needed at the time and that I needed to serve with humility. It didn't take long before I mastered what was given me. I began to create. I worked those props. I created all sorts of items—wings, paper rocks, angel harps—out of paper! I would stay up, sometimes until two or three in the morning. What I was doing was spending quality time with God. I had no internet to teach me how to make items, so I would ask God how to make them and do it at a low cost. It became such a joy to create props out of nothing.

God used my submitted servant's heart to help me create for others. I found out through the whole experience of cancer that he just wanted me to remain connected to him. He used my creativity that he gave me for that purpose. I had to admit I was angry and I was mad. When I began to be creative and serve others, I began to love myself and love God even more. I couldn't continue to be angry about that. God's word began to manifest. God looks on the inside, and man on the outside. My heart, mind, and soul were being healed. Cancer did that for me. I'm better because of what cancer made me face—me from the inside. The Bible says in 3 John 1:2, "I pray that you may enjoy good health and that all may go well with you, even as your soul is getting along well."

The Blank Page

"Be angry and sin not. Do not let the sun go down while you are still angry." —EPH 4:26

Have you ever been angry? Write or draw what made you angry.

_____

_____

_____

_____

_____

_____

_____

_____

_____

_____

_____

_____

_____

_____

I Love Pink

A Lie Reality
1-17-13

What happens to you when you tell the truth?
You change from within
You are able to be free to be yourself
You are powerful

What happens when you lie?
You change from within
Facts are changed
Reality is altered
Truth is covered
People's ethics are forced to be compromised.

Stop the LIE-REALITY
the mixing of both the truth and a lie
The question should be: Why do we lie?
Is the Reality of your life not worth living
for the fear of appearing weak and underachieving?
Who told you that?
The Reality can often just be the process to success.
When you see me wearing a St. John suit, don't hate
Ask: HOW?

Here's the Reality: Upscale RESALE!!!!
The lie would be if I told you
I bought it off the rack and you believed me.
A lie involves people who validate the tale.
What happened to Reality?
What happened to Truth? Excuse me
Please allow me to make mistakes
and learn from them

I Love Pink

> I'm not perfect, I'm human
> I am who I am. It is what it is!!!
> My mama always said, "Tell the truth
> and shame the devil"
> A lie told today is a reality not lived.
> I choose reality, not a lie
> and not a LIE-REALITY, a mix of both.
> The Reality is
> that all things work together for my good.
> Knowing that the Reality may not feel
> or even look right.

I had a wreck one day (January 17, 2013). That day, I realized I had a choice: to speak the truth or a lie-reality. This day, this time, the lie was not mine. It was my fault! This was true. I would pay the cost. I changed to a lane that was occupied and I swiped a vehicle.

The lie? Glad you asked. The other driver was not the owner and was not listed on the insurance. What a lie! "What a tangled web we weave when we practice to deceive"—A LIE-REALITY. I thought he owned the car and had insurance in his name. I could have told a lie and said it was his fault.

I choose to live in reality, to influence the future in a positive way, so when I tell this story, others can live in their reality no matter how bad it looks or even feels.

TELL NO LIE

My Reflection
Lies

I know I've lied. Someone has asked me, "Does this dress make me look fat?" and I've said no. I've lied. I just didn't want to hurt anyone's feelings. We've all lied like that. Some careers are made on lies. Look at some of the fashions. Lies. Mixing plaid with polka dots and calling it "the next big trend." I heard that blue was the color for 2020. "Classic blue is regal, restrained and boundless," according to Kirsi Goldynia of CNN New York. Let's not even talk about politics.

I've lied to myself. I told myself I was not good enough, not a good mother, wife, or person. I didn't need anyone to validate my lies. I did that all by myself. I had this song in my head. That I played on a daily basis. Sometimes it had a different rhythm. After a while I started playing a new song from the word of God: "But you are a chosen people, a royal priesthood, a holy nation, God's special possession, that you may declare the praises of him who called you out of darkness into his wonderful light" (1 Peter 2:9). "For God so loved the world that he gave his one and only Son, that whoever believes in him shall not perish but have eternal life" (John 3:16).

I am royal. I am more than what or who I think I am. I am God's special possession. God sent his son to redeem me even from my selfish, negative thoughts. I have a new song and I will continue to sing it every day. No more lying to myself.

If you ask me my opinion, be ready for my truth.

# The Blank Page

What have you lied about?

_____
_____
_____
_____
_____
_____
_____
_____
_____
_____
_____
_____
_____
_____
_____
_____

I Love Pink

SECTION IV

Humility

The Cross
2012

What kind of love can be found on a cross?
The kind of love that is all consuming.
Imagine pain, pain so severe
you can no longer feel anything
and you are completely drained of energy
You have been nailed to a cross
by bones and ligaments in your wrists and feet.
Every time you need a breath of fresh air
you have to . . . struggle. (demo)
You have bled for hours in the hot sun
from . . . deep . . . deep . . . cuts
into your flesh from special instruments
designed for one purpose . . . mutilation
. . . and the blood has now dripped down
your body and dried into a crusty mess!
YOU LOOK LIKE DEATH . . .
YOU SMELL LIKE DEATH . . .
YOU ARE DEATH
Why would anyone endure this kind of torture?
WHY? . . . Jesus did . . . and . . .
HE did it for LOVE!

His mission was redemption!
His body was just a shell to house his spirit
Until it returned to his father.
The humanity of the moment:
a mere man on a cross for
. . . ALL . . . to see.
The Sadducees marveled at their short-term victory.
Their cruel plot was just a part
of God's plan for man to have an everlasting life
through . . . his son . . . Jesus!!!

I Love Pink

This story would be told
by a crowd of witnesses for generations
and generations forever!!!
"Surely he was the son of GOD"
"If I be lifted up, I would draw all men unto me"
. . . and . . . HE did . . . and . . . HE did it for LOVE!
Jesus, with the help of his father
decided to bear the . . . humility . . . of the cross
knowing he was innocent.
He wanted to SHOW the world what love . . .
LOOKED like.
He never responded with negative words
but with words of compassion
He said, "Father forgive THEM
for they know not what they do."
HIS love for man was so incredible
that when he was placed on the cross
between two thieves
his love was available for both of THEM!
Now . . . these thieves were found guilty
of their crimes
and their punishment was just for that time.
One thief challenged Jesus's deity
saying . . . that if he was the Messiah
he should save himself . . . and . . . them.
The other thief rebuked him, saying
"Don't you fear GOD? HE IS INNOCENT!!!"
and then he asked Jesus if he could join him
in his kingdom.
Jesus responded in love, saying
"Today YOU will be with me in paradise"
Jesus was extending that same (Freedom) life
for BOTH thieves.
. . . but . . . only . . . one . . . of them
asked to go with him.
Unconditional love looks beyond
the outer appearance of man

I Love Pink

past the negative behaviors
which cause so much pain.
Real love embodies potential, hope, and faith
(through . . . pain)
It's a demonstrative action.
We have to do something.
This kind of true/perfect love is what
Jesus was teaching us on that dark day
and . . . on THIS . . . Resurrection Sunday
We must love those who hurt us
from a place deep inside ourselves.

WE CAN! HE DID!! and . . . He did it for love!!!
Jesus was different.
He was talked about and lied on
He was misunderstood by the religious leaders
he was betrayed by one of his closest friends
for what? . . . MONEY?!
Jesus suffered the cross
to redeem man from himself . . . Hallelujah!
He knew what it would cost . . . HIS LIFE
"Oh, how precious is THAT BLOOD!"
and then, when his work was completed, he said
"IT IS FINISHED" . . . period!
and he gave up his spirit . . . back to his father.
What kind of love can be found on the cross?
All consuming . . . unconditional
real . . . pure . . . perfect
What kind of love can be found on the cross?
AGAPE LOVE!!!

My Reflection
"The Cross"

This narration was created for the Agape play **He Did It for Love**. I kinda volunteered to perform. Really, Minister Bobby West persuaded me. I didn't want to minister; I just wanted to work on props. Finally I said okay. I asked him to write something to get me started, and he did. He wrote the first version, then encouraged me to explore and make it mine.

I became one with this narration. I rehearsed it at least twenty times a day. My biggest fear was that I didn't think I could remember it. I found out that this challenge was exactly what I needed. How important it was for me to use words to motivate people, engaging them to understand what Jesus's love was from the cross. I needed to understand what Jesus did for me from the cross, a perspective we never explored in the drama ministry. I rehearsed that narration, a lot of the time on my way home from work. My husband would listen and time me over and over again until it was almost perfect.

It timed at six minutes in the car, but during dress rehearsal on the Saturday before, it all fell apart. I forgot everything. I was so embarrassed. It taught me humility. I was a mess. I couldn't understand. I told Minister West that I'd have it on Sunday. This was how most of our dress rehearsals were. For some odd reason, they were always chaotic. There would always be people missing, actors would get sick, dancers' garments would be damaged, the props would be missing from the set. Then, on the Ministry Sunday, it would come together almost perfectly.

The next day, Easter Sunday, was "showtime." It was on. The dancers and singers were hitting their ministry moments flawlessly. I think we had three speakers and I was the last one, reciting "The Cross." I prayed and felt the power of God. I was ready. My husband said it took nine minutes. All I remembered was walking out on stage, and I stared at that cross and my mind went blank. I forgot what my first line was. I looked at that cross and paused for what seemed like five minutes. I said, "Okay, Jesus, help me." I wasn't nervous. My mind just went blank.

I was a little surprised, and my fears of not remembering came flooding into my mind. Was this to be? Was I too old to remember my lines? Why was this happening? I had to trust God. He was truly my source in that moment. God has a sense of humor. We must walk in humility. When I reviewed the play, the pause was done at just right time to draw the listener's attention to the cross, which took the attention off of me but onto the subject: THE CROSS. The words begin to flow out like a gentle rain. All I had to do was breathe and relax. I didn't know that at the time.

When God is processing something in you and you don't understand, just trust. He knows your beginning from the end. I heard the applause, but I knew it wasn't for me. I was okay with that and I knew it was for the message and the God in me. When I finished reciting the narration, I was physically drained. I had to go by myself to thank God and lie down. I learned about the humility of God that day . . . but it wasn't to be my last moment.

Ha Ha Ha :o)

I Love Pink

Humble

A low estimate of one's importance
Is what the dictionary says.
I'd rather use the word
Modest
Meek
Unassuming, Unpretentious
or
Down to earth.
If you've been a person dealing
with narcissistic behaviors
With an inflated sense of your own importance
You have been
Selfish
Conceited
And egotistic
Then you need to humble yourself
You are important
but
Don't look down on people
who may not have what you have
Or think like you think
Humbleness is a great character to have.
It keeps you balanced and poised.
God honors, rewards, and respects
Those who walk in humility
Be humble

My Reflection
Humility

A few years ago, I was facilitating on a Wednesday evening. Basically I was the one who opened the service, prayed and introduced the speaker, and closed the service. This particular evening, I really didn't want to. I was tired and I was not in the right spirit. Pastor was late. I went through the prayer, read the scriptures. When it came time to introduce the speaker, I noticed that we had a guest. Instead of introducing Pastor, I said "Who's next?" Who's next? I was so wrong and very disrespectful.

Pastor, with her gracious self, grabbed the mic and began to introduce the speaker for the evening. I was so relieved. That meant I could sit and enjoy the word.

Well, the speaker got up and he said, "I need someone with a strong voice to assist me." He looked and pointed to me. My heart dropped. He said, "Come on, sister," and then, "Look at you! You look like a model." I had to read the scriptures for his message while standing in three-inch heels. He would give me a scripture, then say "Read," then stop me and say "Read" again. Then he would say the opposite of what the scripture said and have me verbally correct it. One time I messed up and he had to correct me. One time he was talking about food and he came over and said "sweet potato pie" very loud in my ear. I was so humiliated. I was just a prop for his message. My feet were hurting so bad, but I still had to stand in humility. He thanked me for helping him.

I smiled and said, "You're welcome."

Later that evening, I got quiet. I realized I'd learned a very valuable lesson. I was not a humble servant as a facilitator. Instead, I went through the motions. I was acting. I sounded good, but my heart was not in it. I was selfish. God used the speaker to teach me right in the midst of my wrong. I learned:

- Never underestimate how God will use you.

- Be respectful toward others.

- Always have a servant's spirit.

- Don't just read the scriptures. Always have something to add. Break them down based on your personal experiences and what you learned.

- Have a great introduction ready.

- Be open to be used as a servant with humility.

> "Humble yourselves before the Lord, and he will lift you up" (James 4:10).

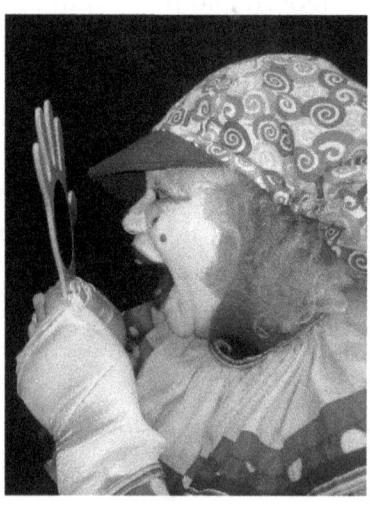

The Blank Page

Humility is the fear of the LORD; its wages are riches and honor and life. —PROV 22:4

Describe a time when you had to stand in humility.

_____

_____

_____

_____

_____

_____

_____

_____

_____

_____

_____

_____

_____

_____

_____

I Love Pink

SECTION V

THE DUNK CHILDREN
&
The Addiction

I Love Pink

Children Are A Blessing
For Rae D'Ann, Phyllissa, and Joshua
4-24-13

When I found out what I had inside of me!
My heart was full of joy
I had life in me.
My blood flowed through you for months.
We were one.
When you moved for the first time,
it felt like gentle butterflies
I laughed.
This feeling only mothers know.
As you grew stronger and larger, so did I.
I could not believe that God allowed
me to carry this creation.
I slept, you moved.
I wondered what you looked like.
Would you be a boy or a girl?
As long as you were healthy, only GOD knew . . .
Rae D'Ann, then Phyllissa . . . two girls
For baby three, your dad prophesied a boy
and his name would be Joshua.
A future doctor, a lawyer
teacher or even a preacher
only God knew what I cherished within.
I carried you for nine months with hope and love.
My hair and nails grew
I could no longer see my feet when I stood.
Destiny was moving and growing in my womb.
so proud was I
To endure sleepless nights
and frequent trips to the bathroom

I Love Pink

The weight gain was just your need
for extra room and nourishment.
Food was an obsession.
Pickles and ice cream tasted real good in baby land.
During the latter months
I had a creative swag when I walked.
Some called it the duck walk.
When your time came to be released
from this increasingly small environment
My body went to work. They call it labor.
PUSH . . . breathe . . . PUSH . . . breathe
Is what they told me to do.
You came into this world
with an innate ability to fight.
Rae-ray was born with her chest bone fractured
Essa was born with white spots on her face
and Josh was born with a club foot
and with a loud cry you cleared your
lungs for the first time.
we became two . . .
Now that you are grown, I want to tell you
to PUSH
to BREATHE
until GOD's glory is revealed in your life.
There's only one like you.
You are fearfully and wonderfully made.
I was used to bring you here
to bring God's glory through your life.
PUSH and BREATHE, my children
the world is waiting on you

I Love Pink

The Actor, the Dancer, & the Singer

My children have gifts that have blessed me

The actor
Made me believe he was who he said he was.
He became the person
with compassion, love, and anger
He made a large egg important . . .
and I cried

The dancer
Made me believe I can dance.
She moves and glides across the floor effortlessly. She loves to groove
and vibe.
When she dances, she gets into a zone.
She made me feel like I can dance . . .
And I did that

The singer
Made me believe she was in the presence of God.
She has a sound
that comes from another place
where I'd rather be.
Where it's safe, peaceful, and full of love . . .
And I went there

My Reflection
Children / Addiction

I really know that my children are a blessing. Two years before my first was born, my husband was addicted to crack. I was addicted to denial. He had an addiction that he tried to hide from me, and I went into denial about how serious it was. I would find little empty brown bottles in the second bedroom. I asked him what they were and he said they were for weed. I accepted his addiction as normal. I should've challenged him. Why was I so weak?

I had quit my job with the state, supposedly to start a family, but the real reason was I didn't want to get fired. I received my 401(k) payout from that job and saved it in our joint bank account. It didn't take long before I found out he'd started withdrawing money out of our savings.

My sister tried to tell me, "Watch your man. He's hanging out with your brother." My brother had no limits when it came to drugs, and I knew that. I went into this denial and a daze. My faith was not strong enough to even pray for him. Looking back, I was so passive. Why didn't I challenge him? I don't know; I just wanted this to stop. It went on for months. I didn't want a confrontation. I was a chicken. I left it between him and God to figure it out. I wrote him a long letter one day. Basically I told him to choose me or the crack, and do it in a hurry. Well, he chose me. He stopped cold turkey and never used again.

During those crack days, I was so confused. I was a good wife. I cooked, cleaned, and made love, but I was competing with this substance that had a tight grip on my husband. He had a wife who was in complete denial and didn't want confrontation for fear that it would escalate into something more. The letter provoked a change in my husband, and what happened next was a miracle. He told me he wanted me and he quit cold turkey. We began to work on our marriage. I began to work on myself physically. I needed something to do. I enrolled in a health club and worked out three times a week. My stresses were relieved. I started taking iron pills. I was feeling great. My body was beginning to take on a different shape.

After he was sober for over a year, I was childless. I thought I was to be the barren woman. I remember taking a shower one day and I was just talking to God. I asked him to bless my womb. I was kinda whining and crying. I was not getting any younger. Well, you have to be ready for your blessing in case God says yes. I had prepared my body. I was working out and building up my endurance. Three weeks after I prayed and whined, I was pregnant with my first child. I was so happy.

Of course, hubby was in disbelief. I was not working at the time and all I did all day was sleep, and I stopped working out. I stopped drinking coffee. I tried to clean, but I got real dizzy. He would leave for work and I would be on the couch, and when he came home, I would still be on the couch. One day he looked at my growing stomach and said, "You *are* pregnant." One early morning I awoke with a serious craving. I was obsessed. I think it was one or two in the morning, but I didn't care. I wanted homemade fries, and I wanted him to cook them. He helped me by just getting up with me. OMG, they were the best fries I ever had! They were hot, greasy, sprinkled with salt and pepper, and drenched in ketchup. I slept like a baby.

A few months passed and we were getting our marriage back on track. Our love was rekindled and we started preparing for the birth of our baby. Rae was born on a very cold day, December 23, 1989. The labor was long and hard and I had to have numerous stitches. She was such a joy. Rae was born with a broken collarbone. I had to keep one of her little arms folded up in an undershirt like a sling for months. We were a family! My husband was a great provider and I was a great wife.

Two years later, I accepted Christ for real. We joined a church and I was pregnant with baby number two, Phyllissa, whom we call Essa because Rae couldn't pronounce her name. She was a quiet and peaceful baby. Essa was born with white spots on her face due to being in a toxic environment before birth. I put ointment on her face every day until her skin cleared.

In another two years, we were pregnant with baby number three, Josh. No one believed me. One day, as I was serving in hospitality, hubby came into the kitchen and said, "I know the sex of the baby and I know what the name will be." I was startled. I grabbed hold of his declaration by faith and refused to hear anything else from anyone. WE WILL HAVE A SON AND HIS NAME WILL BE JOSHUA!

His birth was eventful: his heart stopped beating. I thought we were going to lose him. The doctor had to reach deep inside my womb and stimulate him to get his heart to start beating again. He was born with a club foot. He was long. Every two weeks, we had to take him to Cook Children's hospital to get his cast changed. They were realigning his foot. He would cry in agony.

In four years we had three children, from 1989 to 1993. I made a major decision to have my tubes tied. At the rate we were going, we would have had a team to raise. I know I made the right decision because the next year, 1994, I was diagnosed with breast cancer.

We loved raising our children. We struggled a lot during the early years. Money was tight. I was journaling and writing. We gave them love and ourselves. I was the preschool mom teacher. I taught my children their ABCs, colors, and numbers. One day, after one of my chemo treatments, I remember being so tired. I had to let the children go out to play and get a little air. I would watch them play on the tennis court while I sat on the stairs, watching, almost falling asleep. They never knew how ill I was. They just knew that they were loved and I was present. They gave me strength because they had all of this energy and love. They were just fun to be with, even during discipline times. We read Bible stories to them every night. We kept them close.

I Love Pink

Looking back, I see that it was better that we started a family after the addiction instead of having children during that time. Emotionally I was not ready. My denial and desire to hide any emotions I had during this period would've made it more of a toxic environment for children. I was like a zombie. I hid my anger, resentment, and pain even from myself. When the addiction was kicked, I could finally love again and get back to some type of normal. I was able to truly love my growing family. We realized we were a team.

As they grew older, their gifts began to emerge and blessed me. The dancer is Rae, the singer is Essa, and the actor is Josh. God knew what was best for us earlier than we did. My children are truly a blessing from God.

The Blank Page

"The blessing of the LORD brings wealth, without painful toil for it."
—PROV 10:22

How can you be a blessing?

_____

_____

_____

_____

_____

_____

_____

_____

_____

_____

_____

_____

_____

_____

_____

Addictions

    Drugs
        Love
            Sex
                Crisis
                    Alcohol
                        Work
                            Drama
                                Exercise
                                    Negativity
                                        Chocolate
                                            Money
                                                People
                                                    Stress

Addictions

Everybody has them.
Do you hide yours?
Are they ruining your life quietly?
What's keeping you from being free?
Is it guilt or shame? Or pride?
Be free today. Stop . . . ask God and believe.

The Blank Page

"So if the Son sets you free, you will be free indeed." —JOHN 8:36

What addictions have you been delivered from?

_____

_____

_____

_____

_____

_____

_____

_____

_____

_____

_____

_____

_____

_____

SECTION VI

WORSHIP

A Place
7-14-09

Escape to a place of wonderment
where your heart's desire will be fulfilled.
A place where time has no constraints
it just stops.
You are welcomed and received.
The colors of the rainbow are not labeled
but celebrated with indescribable hues.
Looking up is common.
You are free to stay.
Your spirit is still and at peace.
You know you are part of something
greater than yourself
A place where there's no confusion
And every thought is unified.
Love overwhelms you like a warm blanket.
All you feel is peace and love forever
welcome home to a place . . .

I Love Pink

Hard Work
2012

Hands are scarred
from falling to the ground
trying to break the fall
due to bearing the weight of the cross
Wrists are sore
from large nails being pushed through them
Feet are blistered and callous
from walking a long distance in the hot sun
Back hurting
from deep cuts into the flesh
For you and me
Bruises are on the body from head to toe
But the heart is still full of love
compassion and forgiveness
The head was battered
The beard was ripped from the face
with such force
that it caused an uproar in the crowd
By now the face was unrecognizable
The blood dripped down the body for hours
The soul continued to yearn to be with the father
This hard work was never easy for him.
How can I ask
for what I'm going through to pass me by?
When someone else already endured
the hard work for me
and just for me.

Wake Up

Wake up, wake up
Woman of God
And seek my face
Wake up, wake up
Woman of God
Your troubled heart
Will be healed

Wake up, wake up
Woman of God
Your troubled mind will be filled
I love you, woman of God
Wake up
you are precious.

You Are

You are
my God
You are
my sun
You are
my dance
You are
my life
You Are My Song
You are
my expression
You are my God
You just . . .
You are

When to Worship

Worship when it's trouble
Worship when there's peace
Worship when there's confusion
Worship when there's hope
Worship when you need to release
Worship when you cannot cope
Worship will bring, will bring hope
and fix your scope
Worship using your hands
Worship using your feet
Worship in a dance
Worship on one knee
Worship standing or lying facedown
Worship while singing
make a joyful noise!
When you worship
Defeat must flee!!!

I'll Never Leave You

GOD said: I'll never leave you

God **SAID**: I'll never leave you

God said: **I'LL** never leave you

God said: I'll **NEVER** leave you

God said: I'll never **LEAVE** you

God said: I'll never leave **YOU**

. . . and he never did!

I Love Pink

Covered From

PAIN
CANE
INSANE
AIM
BLAME
GAME
DISDAIN
MAIM
DAME
SHAME
LAME
TAME
WHAT CAME
SAME
PROFANE
CAIN
RAIN

Near the Light

When I stand near the light,
My world is so bright.
I can see clearer.
When I stand near the light,
My spirit takes flight.
When I stand near the light,
I have insight.
When I stand near the light,
My stature has height.
When I stand near the light,
I have might for the fight.
When I stand near the light,
I know everything will be all right.
When I stand near the light,
Jesus is my delight.
When I stand near the light,
He has my plight.
When I stand near THE light,
It's always day and never night.

My Reflection
Worship

I love to worship, just to be quiet in his presence. In the peace of God, the overwhelming sense of knowing you are loved and cared for. Worship sustains me. During these times of forced home confinement and social distancing, it's vital to find God and worship. God has shown himself to me many times. Praying to God is like breathing. I think I'm always praying. I've gotten to a place in life where I realize he is always present. When I need to make a decision, I pray. When I need to repent for something I did or said wrong, I pray.

I can feel God's power and presence when I dance or mime. I have spent time with God, rehearsing. I always seek him on moves. I always want to interpret the words and deliver the message correctly. Recently, one Sunday during the virus crisis, Paula Jackson called me and said she needed to dance. I agreed. Paula and I decided to be brave and go to church and dance. We haven't danced at church for about two weeks. Paula is a worshiper and a giver. She has supported the dance ministry for years. She has provided garments by purchasing them or creating them. She sacrifices her body to dance before God. I have seen this woman dance in and through pain. I've seen this woman return from a red-eye flight early in the morning to dance before God, and then nod off in service.

I've been knowing this powerful lady for years. She's very intuitive. When we dance together, she can anticipate my next move.

She has been a great friend and confidant. I treasure our relationship. Sometimes she needs space, so I give it to her. So when she said she needed to dance, I knew she was on a mission. We were in the back of the sanctuary, which is our place of purging: behind the congregation, but in sight of the praise team. She was on one side and I was on the other. Usually we'll discuss our preplan, the dance order and flags or fabric we'll be using, but not on this particular Sunday. There was no talking, no setting up, and no planning. It was our time to be with God. The presence of God was so sweet that day. She and I were caught up with ministering and being ministered to. After praise and worship, we sat distant from each other as required by social distancing. Once church was over, we chatted for a few minutes and departed, no debriefing. When you just know you touched heaven, there's no extra explaining or dialogue needed. Worship is an experience.

There's another person I've learned from. She taught me how to be graceful in his presence during worship and her name is Eagle Cynthia Corley. This lady taught me how to hold my head up, lift my shoulders up, and minister with grace before God. "Dance your own deliverance," she would say sometimes. She knew that if you're dealing with something, you can take it to God in prayer as well as in dance. Once you dance, you will be delivered from your issues. As a mime, I was awkward and very controlled and forceful. Grace is not like that; it's gentle, but direct. I watched her transform from a little, angry, timid person to a loving, kind, and bold, beautiful soul. I've seen her worship before God until she passed out and dance against doctor's orders. She would spend time in prayer, sweat in the dance room, and teach like a crazy woman.

She looks small, but she's quite heavy. She has muscle weight. I learned that one time during rehearsal. I was trying out a move and I tried to pick her up. It didn't work—she was heavy!

She's powerful in the spirit. We had some real issues and she was fundamental to keeping us dancing together. She would conduct one-on-ones and challenge the women to love one another. There was a time in our dance ministry when it was just the three of us ministering every Sunday: Paula, Cint, and myself. We also would minister for special ministry. One time, Paula and I convinced Cint to dance with a fractured foot, partially sitting down with her special boot. It was a powerful moment when she stood and leaped with her other leg and sat back down. The song was Smokie Norful's "Dear God." We have had some special ministry moments and I gleaned from them all. Thanks, Paula and Cint. I love you guys! Thanks for the lessons.

When I was a young child, I used to be afraid of the dark. I remember one quiet night when I woke up out of a sleep. I saw an illuminated Jesus walking through the middle of my house. He was dressed in white. His face looked like the "typical" Jesus face to me as a six- or seven-year-old. His face was white and glowed. I was frozen, but not really afraid. I never told anyone in my family because I knew they wouldn't believe me and they might think I was cuckoo. I vowed never to tell. From that moment until now, I've always felt someone was with me. Was that my calling? Seeing that, I just simply believed. God was with me then, he was with me when I was going through cancer twice, and he is with me now. His word says he will never leave me, and I believe it because "every word of God is flawless; he is a shield to those who take refuge in him" (Proverbs 30:5).

I thank God for being a powerful presence in my life, for being my shield. Worship helped me get through recovery. When I began to get stronger physically, I began to move and dance. It was my worship to God. I would pray and spend time with him, just talking to him like the friend he is. Sometimes he would speak and I wouldn't listen. Then sometimes I would listen as he spoke. As I began to write, I felt as though I was guided. Like free writing . . . excited about what God was speaking as I wrote.

Worship is like that, whatever position you're in—lying down, sitting, or standing, dancing or not, hands lifted, or on your knees. You're free to worship.

The way I worship may be very different from yours. I have to worship. Sometimes it's not typical. I don't ask for anything. I'm grateful and thankful. He's been too good to me. That is not a cliché—I've got proof. I have battle scars from my victories! I'm known for screaming and running around the church, but I will lay prostrate and humble myself in his presence quietly. I pray that you will lose yourself in his presence and find your destiny and purpose for your life. My worship is for real. Let your worship be for real.

"God is spirit, and his worshipers must worship in Spirit and in truth" (John 4:24).

The Blank Page

God said to Moses, "I am who I am." —EX 3:14

God is . . .

_____

_____

_____

_____

_____

_____

_____

_____

_____

_____

_____

_____

_____

_____

The Blank Page

But he said to me, "My grace is sufficient for you, for my power is made perfect in weakness." Therefore I will boast all the more gladly about my weaknesses, so that Christ's power may rest on me. —2 COR 12:9

What has God's grace taught you?

_____

_____

_____

_____

_____

_____

_____

_____

_____

_____

_____

_____

_____

SECTION VII

WHAT MORE CAN I SAY ...
About My Journey

WHAT MORE CAN I SAY
About My Journey

Over 25 years ago, in 1994, I was diagnosed with breast cancer, and then with colon cancer in 1999. I was an emotional mess. At first I was this angry, sad victim. Why me? was a burning question I wanted an answer to. I went into denial for about a month. I pretended the lump wasn't there until I had to bathe. My husband confirmed the mass in my breast. The lump began to get larger. Eventually it had grown to almost three inches.

I went to the mother of our church, Mother Hornbuckle. I wanted her to know about the mass I'd found. I was crying like a baby. She pulled me into a conference room and felt my breast, which was so comforting. She said, "Okay, enough crying. It's time to go to work." She strengthened me that day. I was able to cry, but also to confront, to begin a new level of faith. I will never forget that moment with her.

When the doctor said, "You have cancer," the realities of my life began to flood my heart. I have cancer. I was frozen. I didn't shed one tear. I wanted to be in control. The number one question that crossed my mind was, will I die? What about my young children? Who will take care of them? My husband will be alone. I was angry, sad, and disappointed. These emotions were no longer dormant in my heart; they were real and tangible, producing fruit. The dormant emotions that I'd masked were erupting. Receiving this news meant I could no longer mask them with a fake smile.

I had to deal with each one from the roots. I had to admit that I was not satisfied with my life. I had not achieved what I wanted. God wanted me to be real with who I had become. I had to answer the question, why? God was warring for my soul. My purpose and destiny were in jeopardy, and my children's destiny as well. It's easy to live in a fantasy world, smiling like you got it going on and dying on the inside. I wanted more for myself and my family, but I didn't know how to achieve it.

There's a saying: "Fake it till you make it!" Well, I got stuck on faking it and never made it. I blamed others for their loving responses to me. I didn't believe people could love so hard. I hid behind the mask, the mask of laughter and happiness. I was fake. I would laugh and smile on the outside, then go home and cry like a baby.

God used that very mask to deliver me, through the art of clowning. I wanted so much to break free and be who I was, happy and full of joy no matter what I was going through. This joy that I have? The world didn't give it to me, and the world can't take it away. I read a couple scriptures one day and now they have become my life's mantra: "A merry heart doeth good like a medicine" and "The joy of the Lord is my strength." I realized joy is the ability to laugh and be happy about life no matter what it brings. So I decided to laugh every day and I understood that this cancer was just a season I was in. The battle was on and all I had to do was have faith and be present.

God did the rest. He says in his word that "the Lord will fight for you; you just need to be still" (Exodus 14:14). I yielded (humbled) myself to the process. I cried and prayed. I was challenged by people I really didn't like, but God placed them in my life to agitate me. God showed me how to love for real. I began to see others through God's eyes and stopped looking at their faults. I took the plank out of my eye. My heart opened up. I could love for real. I must admit there are some people I had to stay away from, but I could still love them at a distance. I was delivered from myself. I realized that he made me to be different. My confidence and boldness emerged. I am a little silly and goofy, but this didn't happen overnight. I began the happy road as I spent time with God and read his word, prayed, and began to dance.

I thought I was crazy for being so happy and full of joy during and after the cancer treatments. I still had some deeper issues buried. Everything was in slow motion. The chemo drugs had me moving slowly, but my spirit was on fire. I had three small children who needed their nurturing mom, a whole mom, and love. I cared for them the best I could. I also had wifely duties. I cared for my husband the best I could and he was very patient with me. I was able to mime for my pastors one afternoon. I just wanted to get this ministry out of my body. I didn't know what to do with this gift. It was the right time and season.

I made the appointment with the assistant. The Pastors had just got news that one of their friends' husbands had died. I was so nervous. During the ministry I saw pain in their eyes. The song was "Precious Lord" by Crystal Lewis. They were in tears when I finished. I was out of breath afterward. I thought I was going to pass out. I was free! The ministry was out of my body. My pastor said, "You messed me up."

I was asked to minister for the launch of the women's ministry a few weeks later. God was breaking me and showing me the power of the gift he had given me. In the following few weeks, I was asked to help by an associate minister, Monita Sharp, to prepare for a birthday party. She was dressing up as a clown for one of her godchildren's birthday parties. I was so elated to help.

She said, "Since you're so excited, start thinking about using this theme to help launch the children's church with a routine." I didn't even think twice. I said okay. That was the push I needed to allow all of this bottled-up happiness-joy stuff to flow out.

Monita was like that for me. She would provoke me out of my comfort zone even if I didn't want to come out and often checked in on me to make sure I was okay. She loved me hard, but very deep. She helped arrange a surprise baby shower for me when I was pregnant with Josh. I was locked out of my own apartment. This was before I was diagnosed with breast cancer. Our girls were very close friends growing up.

Preparing for the children's church launch was like releasing a valve after building up pressure. I had a channel. It was about to blow! God used what was happening on the inside to speak through me in the form of clowning and mime. My self-esteem was lifted. I was a clown with happy, bright makeup on the outside, but it was the same on the inside—bright and happy. I was full of joy on the inside and outside, and it was real! I had a purpose. I could love. I found makeup, a clown costume, shoes etc. It was like it came out of nowhere. God was supplying what I needed: Manna from heaven! What is this? It was amazing.

I had a nearly two-hour program for the launch of children's church. One of the mothers said, "You should do birthday parties and get paid." I took her advice. I took out an ad in *DFW Child* magazine and started getting booked for parties and making money. I also began to mime more. It was my worship. When I mimed, I felt such gratitude. I learned about grace through some dance movements and God's grace through faith. Life was good . . . until the next hit.

I was diagnosed with colon cancer in 1999. Before the diagnosis, I began to notice a lot of blood every time I went to the restroom. I prayed and prayed, and I know I heard God say, "Don't look at the blood." While I was being operated on, they found out that my gallbladder was full of stones and my ovaries were inflamed. The doctors removed those organs. I had three surgeries in one. I was very sick. My children were so sad to see their mom in that sick state in the hospital. They didn't know how to interact with me and barely looked me in the eyes. Their expressions were so gloomy. It was a difficult visit for us all. I had a lot of visitors, but I was so doped up, I slept through most of the visits.

When I got the colon cancer diagnosis, I was about to transferred to another building to be a trainer on another level at my job. I told my boss, "You don't know what I'm capable of." I was told, "We already know of your work." My boss advised me to have my surgery and return when I was stronger, and that was comforting. I was out for about six weeks. The pathologist said they got it all! I returned to work

I Love Pink

and trained hundreds of people.

I clowned and mimed as I was teaching. I love teaching. I made the classes fun. I would piggyback on a lot of my students' stories and make them apply to the training course they were about to embark upon. I remembered sitting in dull classes, falling asleep while listening to monotonous trainers. I was determined not to be dull and to be a moving target.

I was booked for a birthday party with a fellow clown about eight weeks after I my surgery. I was full of joy, so overjoyed that I lost my footing and slipped. I did a split I didn't stretch for. I was in so much pain, I had to excuse myself to make sure I was all right. I thought I'd popped something from the inside. I really had to talk to God and my body. I returned and continued, but I was very careful. We served about fifty children that day.

God used cancer to deliver me from myself. He gave me a platform to speak from. Cancer saved and enriched my life. It seems strange to admit that. God uses the foolish things to confound the wise. It has been an amazing journey. I still have trials. I'm a work in progress. I will never be 100 percent physically, and I'm okay with that because God is my strength when I'm weak. This old body can out-praise-and-worship any millennial! My church is where I find joy through being a humble servant. God is where I find peace with who I am. I find myself reflecting on how I was placed over the dance team and basically over the fine arts. I have written plays and choreographed dances that I never went to school to learn. God had me learn by observing. I believe the arts are another way for God to speak to his people. My children are actors, singers, and dancers. When they had their rehearsals for plays and other performances, guess who volunteered to help with props? I learned a lot and was able to impart my knowledge to others at my church.

I've had numerous jobs over the past twenty years. During every job I've had, I've been able to work on this book. That's a blessing. I know that this book had to be birthed. There was a season when I was only working every six months. Seeds were sown from a famine household. We gave offerings when we needed to pay bills. We trusted God. We still gave of our time and resources with a grateful heart. During those times of unemployment, I realized I was available to be a real mom for my children and a wife for my husband. I cleaned my house, cooked, and received my children after school. I know that when I'm weak and I depend on God, he is my strength. I know that with God, all things are possible. Why did I share that? I just want people to know that when God blesses, it's in his timing. There's a prerequisite: he wants us to stand in our faith, acknowledge our issues, and trust him through the process until the end. There are lessons that we have to learn and only he controls the what—it's tailor-made. What a great God to serve.

What more can I say? This cancer journey has been overwhelming at times and rewarding at times. I could have never imagined that such good could come out of a ruthless diagnosis like cancer. I have learned to be who God has called me to be. I have had people in my life helping and provoking me to greatness. I'm empowered and full of life. Writing this book revealed even more facets of my character that

I needed to explore.

The Blank Page

"No temptation has overtaken you except what is common to mankind. And God is faithful; he will not let you be tempted beyond what you can bear. But when you are tempted, he will also provide a way out so that you can endure it. —1 COR 10:13

What has been the hardest transition in your life?

_____
_____
_____
_____
_____
_____
_____
_____
_____
_____
_____
_____
_____
_____
_____

I Love Pink

SECTION VIII

Worry

I Love Pink

What If?
12-16-03

I lose all of my hair
I lose a breast
I lose weight
I fight thoughts of dying
I can't sleep at night
I throw up a lot
I become too ill to get out of bed
I can't take care of my family
I can't take care of myself
My fingernails turn black
My tongue develops purple spots
like a German shepherd dog
All my body movements are in slow motion
I can't even form words to speak
I can't pray
But what I can say is Jesus
What if all these things happen to me
And I'm still here?
What if they happen to
YOU?

Woulda, Coulda, Shoulda
3-21-13

How can worrying help?
Would haves, should haves, and could haves
Repeating events over and over and over
in your mind
hoping to figure out what went wrong.
You create pessimistic, negative baggage
to reopen again and again.
Would haves, should haves, and could haves
It's almost like doing the same thing over and over expecting a
different result.
Psychologists call that crazy.
Once the experience occurs, it's over.
Why live in the past in the present?
Only God knows your end from the beginning.
Stuck on
would haves, should haves, and could haves?
Move on.
You wear your worry like a badge. You proud of that? It's really sad
to see you carry
something you can bury.
Do you want people to say, "Wow, they really care?
Oooh, let's give them a trophy." Clap clap
You're a worrywart, a nag.
This condition is like
when a baby has too much food in its stomach
and some of it comes up, only to be consumed again. It's called
rumination.
You are now an adult
just ruminating falsehoods
that are killing your destiny
and trying to change the past with a thought.

I Love Pink

Can you add one day to your life by worrying?
What you will add is sickness and disease.
The depression puppet master is waiting on you.
Do you want to wear a white jacket
you can't get out of?
Take a pill and chill until the end?
The word says think on things that are above. Positive things that
bring you joy.
Gazing at a lazy lake, a sunset
listening to your favorite music
or something noble and good.
Cast your cares to someone who can help.
Jesus said, "Take my yoke
It's easy
and learn my ways."
Instead of
would haves, should haves, and could haves
You can think about the possibility
of what I will have.

My Reflections
Woulda, Coulda, Shoulda

Being overwhelmed with life caused me to worry. I allowed my mind to over-process. When I started this cancer-and-emotion journey, I realized I was a quiet worrier. On the outside I was smiling, but on the inside I worried. I had to release the control to God. I questioned everything. Why did I get cancer? Am I gonna die?

That question was the number one thing I worried about. I was told I had the best doctors and treatments, but still I worried. I prayed, worshipped, danced until I finally surrendered cancer to God. Nothing mattered at this point. My faith had grown. I knew that to be absent from the body is to be present with God. This surrender was not instant. My faith needed time to develop. I worked on my faith. I spent time with God and myself. My mind, heart, and spirit came into agreement with God's word and his will for my life.

When I hit the four-year mark after my breast cancer diagnosis and got colon cancer, I still had faith to believe he had a plan for my life and death was not it, at least not yet. I asked God what else I needed to learn. When the five-year mark after the colon cancer diagnosis came, I was so happy. It came around 2004. I went on my first cruise with my husband. It was our eighteenth anniversary and my birthday celebration. We had the time of our lives. We saw a lot of blue water, sunrises, and sunsets. We loved on each other, held hands, walked, talked, and ate good. There were no worries.

> "Let us not become weary in doing good, for at the proper time we will reap a harvest if we do not give up" (Galatians 6:9).

Don't let weariness grow. Acknowledge it and allow God's word to overrule your emotions. Life will cause you some discomfort, but trust God through it all. He knows what's best for you. I'm not writing this just to be writing—this is the life I lived and the faith I have.

The Blank Page

Therefore I tell you, do not worry about your life, what you will eat or drink; or about your body, what you will wear. Is not life more than food, and the body more than clothes? Look at the birds of the air; they do not sow or reap or store away in barns, and yet your heavenly Father feeds them. Are you not much more valuable than they? Can any one of you by worrying add a single hour to your life? —MATT 6:25–34

What are (were) you worried about?

_____

_____

_____

_____

_____

_____

_____

_____

_____

_____

I Love Pink

Say This Prayer

I decree and declare that I will not allow

worry to control my life,

and I will live in peace in Jesus's name.

AMEN!

I Love Pink

SECTION IX

Wonder

I Love Pink

Little Flower
6-2-09

What type of flower can handle any storm
with grace?
Even Rain, Hail, Wind, or Fire?
THIS little flower can weather it all.
An innate ability to change things
from deep within . . .
When the world has cast an evil shadow . . .
THIS flower has the power to expose and annihilate.
Look at THIS flower
it's small in stature
but don't be fooled or confused.
When THIS flower opens its petals, demons flee
THIS flower is the most beautiful
of all the flowers in nature.
THIS flower is even respected by insects
because they're assured they will be protected
by its leaves.
They're careful not to crush the soft petals
when they crawl past.
No one knows that with every storm
THIS little flower
loses its fragile petals . . . with great joy!
For it knows
that with the new birth, THIS flower
will become much larger, more vibrant, and stronger
than before
with colors that are inspired by GOD
and cannot be described by mankind.
THIS little flower has great faith
that can move all obstacles out of its path
with weapons made by the creator.

I Love Pink

Love drips from the tips of its petals
like dewdrops on a new, fresh spring morning
and flows
on every creature it comes into contact with.
THIS little flower
with power, faith, strength, and love
embodies the person of _____.

Cancer

C: Complex//Calm//Cool//Connected

A: Anger//Angels//Attitude//Alive

N: Never//Next//No//Nice

C: Cancel//Childlike//Change//Calm

E: Encounter//Enter//Explore//Exchange

R: Review//Rejuvenate//Remember//Revelation

I Love Pink

Sunflower
1996

A flower that can stand (endure)
extreme heat and grows better in the sun.
The more heat, the taller it will become.
A sunflower will reproduce many seeds in its lifetime
and can be replanted and replanted.
This sunflower that can withstand a lot of heat
also needs water to survive.
This special flower
needs a lot of water and a lot of heat.
Some people need a lot of heat and a lot of water
to reproduce blessing or seeds in their lives.
Once a seed from a sunflower is planted
it needs constant and consistent attention.
We as Christians need the same attention
by washing ourselves with the word.
Just like the sunflower, our life is never over
as long as we plant seeds
Seeds that bring life
and provoke someone to rethink and begin to live
Wisdom for the young that dismisses the old cliché
"Do as I say but not as I do."
Instead, live
and do as I do because I do what is right!
There are many seeds inside each one of us.
Is it harvest time?
Plant your seeds and watch them grow.
Are you a sunflower? Are you a son flower?

My Reflections
Wonder

"Sunflower" was one of my first poems. My family was going through a lot of transitions (hell). The heat was on in my life, shining down real heat on me and my family. I wrote because I needed resolve. I knew it was only a season, but it was still hot. We moved from Arlington to Fort Worth. I was not working at the time and we needed so much. Josh, my youngest, was born with a club foot in 1993. He had frequent doctor visits to correct his foot. Plaster (a cast) was applied, I think, every two weeks to keep his foot in place until surgery. He cried every time we went in. They physically turned my baby's foot from a club position. He had a surgery that permanently corrected his foot when he was about a year old, around April of 1994. He slowly learned how to walk after the surgery.

I was diagnosed with cancer in November of 1994 and I had the surgery in December. Then I began chemo early in 1995, followed by radiation treatments. Our HEART TO HEART women's ministry had just begun. I was asked to mime during the launch in 1996. During one of those meetings, Pastor gave out her gifts as usual. My name was called and I received a box of pencils and two small journals. I was overjoyed. I won something and my name was called!

I vowed that I would use these small journals to write down my thoughts. I treasured those journals. We were living in a duplex and I was happy to have grass in the front and back yard. I used to love to eat sunflower seeds. Out of curiosity, I began to plant a few. I soon noticed how they grew tall and firm in the sun. Those flowers needed more sun than water. They are a hearty plant with large stalks and large leaves. Right in the middle of this amazing flower are seeds to eat or plant. I started reflecting on my life and writing. I was amazed about the revelation. My life was like this sunflower. I realized that even though we were going through a lot in that season, we were still growing under the intense pressure and the reward always reproduced something positive. I did not grow weary. Weariness was definitely present, but it didn't grow and overtake me. Eventually I would decorate our next apartment with sunflowers everywhere!

I learned about grace. There was no way out except through. GLORY! I had to be the strength for my son and my family. I had a lot of help from my dear mom. She would let us borrow her car, give us money, and even buy us groceries. I had to bear the suffering of raising a family during hard times. I was the preschool teacher. To add structure to our days, I taught them their basics. It was a joy to be with my children during this time. We would have classes: ABCs, numbers, writing, simple math, art, and PE. We would go outside and walk, run, or just dance. Lunch was around noon, and then a nap for two hours. Sometimes they would actually sleep. We would watch a couple of cartoons after naptime. Free time was just playing in their room. I would transition for dinner and do some housework.

This went on for about six months. I loved that duplex. It was home. I worked hard as a homemaker and loved being a stay-at-home mom. Our landlords were very gracious and loving, but we couldn't afford the rent. We were asked to move out. They were losing money.

We moved to Woodhaven, "the hood." That's where I conquered cancer and God showed me his wondrous ways. We moved into a one-bedroom apartment on the top floor. It was a sunny and bright place. We live there for a couple of years. God just cared for us while we lived there. People gave us money, strangers bought us food, and friends cared for our children when I was having treatments. I cried when we moved. That place was transforming. Times were about to get harder. HE IS A WONDER!!

> "He performs wonders that cannot be fathomed, miracles that cannot be counted" (Job 5:9).

I Love Pink

The Place

This was the place where I was sick
This was the place where I went through
chemo and radiation
This was the place where I slept
This was the place
where I got my hair cut in the bathroom
This was the place where I felt loved
This was the place
where I received support from my church
This was the place where my joy was restored
This was the place where I healed
This was the place
where God showed me his strength
This was the place where love flowed through me
This was the place
where I had to give control over to God
This was the place
where God showed me his wonders
This was the place where I worshipped
This was the place where I danced
This was the place where I nurtured my children
This was the place where I was a wife
This was the place where my faith increased
This was the place
where giving up was not an option
This was the place
where I went to school with my children
This was the place
where I became a Head Start representative for a center
This was the place
where God showed me how great he is
This was the place

The Blank Page

Let us not become weary in doing good, for at the proper time we will reap a harvest if we do not give up. —GAL 6:9

What was the hardest transition in your life?

_____

_____

_____

_____

_____

_____

_____

_____

_____

_____

_____

_____

_____

_____

_____

SECTION X

Fear, Joy & Rejection

False Evidence Appearing Real

The evidence in my mind is real
When I'm afraid I can't deal
My mind tells my body to freeze
I can't I can't I can't
My heart began to race
my breathing becomes heavy
my thoughts are controlled by
FALSE EVIDENCE APPEARING REAL
I have proof
What I feel is real
You see me shaking
You see me crying
You see me frozen
I can only feel fear
What makes it false?
When confusion and doubt reign
a life of fear leads to loneliness, disease, and death
Am I sick?
You accept that fear is your punishment
You lower your heart
and lower your expectations in life
You're not enjoying life abundantly
FALSE EVIDENCE APPEARING REAL
What can break this vicious circle?
His Love and Strength

My Reflections
Fear

Fear is real. It's how we choose to respond.

Do we run? Or do we hide? We're supposed to stand in the midst of fear, knowing that God is with us. Do we want to continue to be afraid or do we want to conquer our fears? We can be fearful of a lot of different things. Some phobias are disabling. Claustrophobia is the fear of small spaces. The fear of clowns, coulrophobia, can cause people to be hospitalized. The most common phobias are acrophobia, the fear of heights; trypanophobia, the fear of needles; aerophobia, the fear of flying; and carcinophobia—the fear of cancer.

When I found out I had cancer, I was afraid and I had questions about my future. I wondered if I was going to live or die. I decided to let God take over. This was not automatic. I had to pray and process this fear. I finally realized that cancer was too much for me to handle on my own. I knew I had an adversary, but I also knew God had all power. God did not give me the spirit of fear, but of power, love, and a sound mind. I found myself at peace and a willing participant. I quoted scriptures, prayed, and cried until I finally had a breakthrough. I surrendered the fear of cancer totally over to God. Peace came over me and I began to live.

My fear wasn't limited to cancer. My husband and I visited Hawaii in 2019 for the second time. I was finally ready to deal with the other fears: heights and health issues. I really didn't know how deep these fears were. They weren't debilitating, but I needed to address them in order to move on with my life. Why was I so afraid of these things? I would sometimes drive over a bridge and get a feeling like the bridge was going to collapse. I remember driving in Houston and going around this high bridge because I was so afraid. The GPS in the car went crazy and my family was a little confused. It took us an hour to get back on the correct route. I remember that sometimes, when I worked on props at church, I would ask someone else to climb the ladder to hang fabrics. Enough was enough!

Diamond Head in Hawaii is the eleventh-highest rated tourist attraction in Waikiki. It offers beautiful scenic views while hiking eight miles up 560 feet on an uneven trail. I talked myself out of hiking the trail two years ago. I was overly concerned and worried about the condition of my heart and my knee and the "what ifs." What if I passed out? What if I had to be airlifted to the hospital? What if I fell up or down the stairs? What if my knee began to hurt? All of these fears and worries began to flood my mind. I had allowed them to grow to an excess that left me paralyzed emotionally. I didn't want to do anything that involved heights, and I really didn't want to deal with anything that challenged me. Hmm . . . could that have been the real issue for me in life? Not wanting to deal with anything and just become numb? Trying to escape life's issues on my own terms?

As I began walking two years ago, I felt a little uneasy in my breathing, which I often feel when I dance. What was the difference this time? I made up my mind that I couldn't get through it and I told my husband I couldn't walk up all those stairs. From my point of view, looking back, it seemed unachievable. The altitude was different from what I'm used to. The air was thinner. I'm in fairly good health, but I had found an excuse not to continue.

I stuck to that position and made my husband agree. I told him that he could go ahead without me. Of course he didn't. I left with the idea of coming back and finishing this hike one day. I just didn't know how soon it would be. During that moment, I chose not to process.

In 2019, my husband decided he wanted to visit Hawaii again. He declared that we were gonna hike all the way to the top. I agreed. I'd finally made up my mind to do it. I encouraged myself—no matter what, I was going to complete the hike. We invited our children to come along, but they were in the process of getting new jobs. We postponed the trip for a month, but they were still unavailable to travel with us. We booked our flight and stuck to it.

The day of the hike was great. The weather was perfect. I had a positive attitude. We ate a big breakfast. I had on the right clothes. I was ready to conquer my fears. I took an ibuprofen and prayed softly and began "the ascent."

When I reached the place where I'd stopped two years before, I was feeling really great. My husband asked me if I wanted to stop. I said no. The surface was smooth, but inclined. In about a hundred yards, the pavement changed to an uneven surface that caused me to adjust my footing as I walked. I was in no pain. I could feel the air getting a little thin due to the altitude change. I began to watch my breathing, making sure I just relaxed and enjoyed the hike and views.

After another hundred yards, it was time for a little break. I still had no pain. After that break, people were coming down from the crater, speaking words of encouragement.

"Keep going."

"You can make it."

"Take the path on the left."

I actually heard one person say, "It's not that hard." I encountered large puddles of water that I had to figure how to step around. I began to hold on to the railing and broke a nail trying to support myself on the walls. People were passing me, running up. People were running on the way down. Models passed us, looking fierce. Their makeup was light and they had on matching workout gear. Mothers were carrying their babies, and young toddlers were hiking as well. The old, the young, the fearless—and me, full of faith but cautious. At this point I wanted to stop. I began to quote scriptures.

"Let this mind be in you that is also in Christ Jesus."

"God did not give me the spirit of fear, but of power, love, and a sound mind."

"You came that I may have life and life more abundantly."

The endorphins kicked in and I got overjoyed. When we reached a staircase that contained ninety-nine stairs, I took a deep breath. I remembered that a lot of people behind me were eager to reach the top. I didn't want to hold up the line. I held on to the rails and pulled myself up those steps. Still, I was in no pain. I looked real strange, and I felt just as strange, but I didn't care how I looked or how I felt at the time. I had my eyes on the prize, which was completion.

Then . . . it was tunnel time. I almost lost it in there, but I kept quoting scriptures. It wasn't dark, but a little narrow, and the quality of the air was different. It felt like I was inhaling dirt. I heard my husband behind me, breathing just as hard but still encouraging me.

We finally reached the point where we could go left or right. I was breathing hard and sweating. The left stairs were supposed to be a little easier, the right stairs were supposed to be harder, and it was another ninety-nine stairs straight up. I had nothing more to prove . . . we went left. After the stairs was a platform we could step on that was slightly extended off the crater, where we could take pictures and see the views. I passed on that. It didn't look safe to me. There was limited railing and too many people. I was okay with that since we were basically at the top.

When I turned around to see how far and how high I was, I might have lost it if it wasn't so beautiful. I was amazed. It felt wonderful! I still had to climb a few more steps to reach the bunker where the guns used to be during World War II. When I reached that point, I was surrounded by people vying for room to take pictures. The view was spectacular and worth every emotion I went through to get there. We spent about 30 minutes up there. I was elated and very proud of myself. I have been afraid of a lot over the years. This particular fear was real. In order to overcome this fear, I had to place myself in a fearful situation and process my way out. I learned:

- I had to realize what I was fearful of.

- I had to make up my mind to complete the hike and face my fear.

- I had to dispel every "what if" and make no more excuses.

- I had to declare God's word.

On the way down from the crater, we began to encourage others. I was still careful, but it was easier coming down. I still had no pain. I found myself laughing and thanking God and my husband for all his encouragement.

Once I made it down the mountain, I embraced my husband and cried. I exhaled, then shouted, "I did it!" This was a profound lesson in my life as I complete this book.

FACE YOUR FEARS! Remember, "I can do all things through him who give me strength" (Philippians 4:1).

The Blank Page

For the Spirit God gave us does not make us timid, but gives us power, love and self-discipline. —2 TIM 1:7

What are your fears?

_____

_____

_____

_____

_____

_____

_____

_____

_____

_____

_____

_____

_____

_____

My Dance

I dance to live
I live to dance
I dance to reveal
I dance to enhance
I dance to heal
I dance to prance
I dance to feel
I dance to establish a stance
I dance a great deal
I dance with a glance
When I dance, I'm real
I dance everyday
I dance when I'm happy
I've danced when I'm sad
I dance to change from being sad
I feel God when I dance
I dance in my bare feet
Lately I dance in shoes to protect my aging feet
I've danced in the street
I've danced on a beach
I've even danced on a mountain at 560 feet
I've danced to entertain
I dance to worship
I've danced as a mime
I have happy feet
I've dance with the old and the young
I can dance slow
I can dance fast
I can dance high
I can dance low
I can dance in a circle
I can dance using my arms
I can dance with grace

I Love Pink

I've danced for warfare
I've danced for victory
I've danced to drums
I've danced facing the wind
I've danced with the wind at my back
I dance to a different beat
I've danced with strangers
I've danced with friends
I've danced with God
I've danced with my man while holding hands
I love to dance with my children
When I dance, I make room
When I dance, I move my arms
Everything is all right when I dance
Hearts are touched when I dance
Something happens to me when I dance
I can dance in a group
I can dance all alone
I love to dance with fabrics
I can dance in my mind
I can dance in a chair
I love to dance for God
I love to dance with God
I live to dance
I love to dance
This is my dance

My Reflections
Joy / Rejection

Having cancer treatments left me physically depleted. I remember having a strong urge to move, but I moved like a zombie, the dancing dead. I had been still for too long. I started dancing and moving daily. It felt so good, I kept moving until I had routines. This was my happy place. I felt joy when I danced. I wasn't a trained dancer; I just wanted to move.

K & K Mime Ministry was one of my early mentors. They ministered to my spirit. When I saw them, I was overwhelmed and knew this ministry art form was what I wanted to do. They are the fathers of gospel mime. I had an opportunity to meet them in 1998 at one of our church conferences. They were so humble and gracious. They told me to just keep doing it. Over the years I have choreographed numerous mimes and dances. I never had any formal training. I just like to move and tell a story. I have written plays and narrations, and attended plays, dance recitals, ballets, and other performances. I realized I was learning something from each performance.

When I started to regain my strength, I used to hang around the dance team at my church. I once overheard someone say that maybe a large person shouldn't be one of the dancers in the front. I took that in and shut down. I felt rejected. I was hurt. I allowed someone else's opinion to determine my attitude about myself. I was stuck emotionally. This emotion was powerful. It bled and merged into feelings of low self-esteem and depression. I had to come out of that stage because there was this driving force inside of me pushing me to keep moving. And I did.

I Love Pink

I used to volunteer on the dance team. This team was comprised of trained dancers. A few of them had tried out for the Dallas Cowboys cheerleaders. They knew all of the dance terminology, leaps and turns and all that. I was the one who would check in with them on Sundays before services. I made sure they had safety pins, tied their belts, delivered their CDs to the sound booth. It was a season of humility and service. I loved helping them and had no idea I was prepping for a promotion.

I asked the dance leader at the time, Minister Karen McDaniel (my old landlord), if I could just rehearse with them so I could stay in shape for mime. She was so kind and gentle with me. She said, "Sure, just stay in the back." I remember those times. I felt like this stiff giant. The rehearsals were on Thursday nights from 7:00 to 9:00 p.m. I remember one night, after months of serving and watching them rehearse, when she told the whole group to welcome me as a new member. I was so surprised. I was not expecting to be one of the dancers. I was just happy being around them, serving with humility.

Rejection can leave you empty and paralyzed emotionally. Even if it's not intentional, it's how you interpret it. God knew the plans he had for me. The plan was to be healed and dance. My size doesn't negate my ability to minister. I had to learn that and teach that to someone else. I realize the driving force that kept me moving was passion, another emotion. If you don't have passion for dance or anything else, you won't be effective. It fuels gifts. Passion will cause you to practice longer, past the point of exhaustion.

Dealing with rejection was a great lesson for me and one I had to teach someone else. I remember a larger woman who also felt rejected. I invited her to the mime ministry. She mimed and did praise and worship, then became a prophetess and ministered with flags. Her name was Amanda. She is now ministering with the angels. Don't tell me what God won't do or who he won't use to minister. He's used a donkey before. Glory!

A Merry Heart

Something to treasure
Out of the abundance of the heart
the mouth will speak
Something clever and unique
Create in me a clean heart
free from the pressure of my aggressor
Light as a feather, ready to be a server
Never a depressor but always a pleasure
Measure out a heart eager to love
Whether it's been wronged or treated better
The medicine is always good
Take a dose every day
And keep your heart merry.

The Blank Page

The joy of the lord is my strength. —NEH 8:10

What makes you happy.

THE BLANK PAGE

For the Spirit God gave us does not make us timid, but gives us power, love and self-discipline. —2 TIM 1:7

Describe a time when you felt rejection.

___

___

___

___

___

___

___

___

___

___

___

___

___

___

___

___

SECTION XL

Death Aging

I Love Pink

A Father's Love
6-24-09

A father's love knows no boundaries
His love is deeper than the ocean
His arms wide
He'll carry you when you are weak
And stand with you
when you cannot speak
He'll laugh with you and cry with you
With every new birth you bring
He sees a glimpse of himself
For every victory you have
he'll be your cheerleader
And when life overtakes you,
He'll be there
With a shoulder to lean on and to cry on . . .
So remember this
A father's love knows no boundaries
It will go on and on and on . . .
Just like Daddy's love should

My Reflections
A Father's Love

~

This poem was written with love for my stepdad, who had just passed on the day after Father's Day.

I wanted to connect with him so much. I would visit with him and just sit with him. We would talk about the kids, his health, and current events. He was a man of few words, but he loved my mom, my siblings, and me. He had a quiet strength that I admired and I never got a chance to tell him. On my wedding day he gave me hug that was so overwhelming. He said he did that because I was "shaking like a leaf." That's the kind of man he was. He knew exactly what to do and what to say at the right time.

It was hard to call him Daddy, but not because we never felt love from him. We tried, and he knew we loved him. I guess we couldn't call him Daddy in part because we had our daddy in our lives already, from before the divorce. It was an emotional connection we had with our birth dad. We were hurt and wanted to keep what little connection we had with our dad. We loved our natural daddy, missed him, and wanted to protect our mom and ourselves. I think we used the "daddy" name to control the situation.

When he first came into our lives, he said we could call him Adam, but Mama demanded that we call him "Mr. Adam" out of respect. This man took on a woman and her four children. He provided for us. He worked two jobs to support and raise us. He was committed to us. He loved us.

During my teenage years, we spent a lot of time in the house together.

I Love Pink

My mom would attend gambling parties on the weekends, and sometimes she took me. I used to hate those parties—all the drinking, cussing, and smoking. That was no place for a young girl. I used to be nearby, sleeping on a couch, not out of sight or hearing range. I think it was because of him that I started staying home. Most nights I would watch TV in my room. He made sure I had something to eat. I was kinda on my own, but he was in the house. I would see my mom on Sundays or even on Monday morning before school. It was a lonely time.

He took me to my first concert: Ike and Tina Turner! I had a great time, but I don't think he did. He was gone a lot, but I know he was close by, watching. Some of the topics of the songs were way too provocative for my tender ears.

The first set of grandkids called him Paw-Paw, and it caught on. The name was endearing and loving, and the family loved using it. In writing this short poem, I was able to honor him in a lasting way and heal from the guilt of not being able to express to him how much he meant to me. On Father's Day I cooked chicken alfredo in his honor. He said, "I just don't have an appetite." I sat with him in his den and we just engaged in small talk. I kissed him goodbye and told him I loved him. He told me he loved me too.

On the next day, Monday, my niece called to let me know that Paw-Paw had collapsed and was rushed to the hospital. He was being worked on in the back and they were waiting on the doctor's report. When I was on my way to the hospital, I called Jasmine back because I needed to know where I was going. I looked at my phone and the time was 10:19 p.m. We got to the hospital's emergency waiting room and waited for what seemed like hours.

The doctors finally came to talk to the family, but in my heart, I knew he was gone. My mom just sat there with so much grace. I don't recall seeing her cry. The hospital staff moved his body to a room in the back of the hospital. As I approached his lifeless body lying on the hospital bed, I lost it. I shouted, "Thank you!" I didn't care how it came out. I

I Love Pink

cried for a little while. We had prayer and then went home. Adam Dobson was here and made an impact on my life, and he will remain in my heart forever. I love you, Daddy Paw-Paw. I'm forever grateful for you.

I Love Pink

A Poem for My Mama
3-5-13

My mama helped me to be a woman
she taught me to respect myself
she allowed me time to find me
She kept me close to teach me to be careful
The teenager that didn't understand
Rebelled
All I did was yell
Mama said, "Yell, and you will go to hell
Your days will be short."
One night I saw stars and heard a bell
That ended my yell
My mama loves me
I'm the baby girl, the spoiled one
The last one left at home
She taught me how to love
And to be loved
She taught me how to cook
She taught me how to clean
She taught me how to learn
To be responsible and not codependent
She taught me how to pay bills
And to plan for a rainy day
I learned to be the mother that she was not
She taught me to pray, have faith, and trust God
And to be patient when things go crazy
This poem is for my mama.

My Reflections
A Poem for My Mama

This was the second attempt to write a poem for my mama. The first one was not well received and understandably so. The title was referring to a female dog. It was way too strong and disrespectful. I wanted to honor her with love and respect, and without any confusion.

My mom was my rock and the rock for our family. She kept us together. My mom created opportunities for the family to commune. She actually had her home remodeled so we could all fit and be together during the holidays. She was the queen of hospitality! She loved to entertain. If someone visited her home, she would make sure they had something to eat or drink. Sometimes she would have a little gift for them.

Annie Mae was a strong black woman. She grew up during hard times in the Depression era. She was raised by her aunts, uncles, and father. I have grown to understand her need to gather things. She grew up wanting and without. My mom is a collector of things such as clowns, clothes, colored glass, owls, and food. She never allowed me to look down on myself. When I thought I wanted to be a model, she enrolled me in a school in Dallas, but it turned out to be just to build up my self-esteem. When I wanted to dance, cheer, take pictures, or even act, my mama provided an opportunity.

During my teenage years, our relationship was a little distant. She spent a lot of time away from home at gambling parties, and I rebelled against her most of the time. Looking back, I see that we were both growing.

I Love Pink

I loved my mom. She was the type of mom who loves deep and hard. When cancer hit my life, she was right there by my side, and she stayed there throughout my recovery. Since I wasn't working and my husband worked during the day, she persuaded me to stay at her home so she could take care of me directly. It got to be a little overwhelming and I went home to be with my family after a week. I basically slept for most of the days I was there.

I had to write a special poem for my mama. I watched her health decline over the years. She went from a large statue of a woman to a small and delicate woman. I knew her time was approaching. I had been preparing for a few years. One day a few years before, we were sitting at the table, talking. My niece and my sister were over visiting. I forgot what we were talking about, but my mom looked at me and said, "Phyllis, it is what it is." Something hit me from the inside. That statement didn't fit into what the conversation was about, but I knew it was her way of telling me, "Phyllis, I do love you, but my thinking is off. I can't articulate like I used to. Please just accept the state that I'm in mentally and physically." She was diagnosed with dementia and the symptoms began to surface. There would be visits when she would just look at me. Then there would be times when she was very talkative.

One time, she came over to my house. In my backyard we have a large pecan tree. I picked some off the tree and put them in a bowl. Picking pecans basically means we sit around the table to crack and clean them. We enjoyed that time. She was a master at picking pecans.

After one of my emotional visits to her house, she was asleep and it looked like she had passed on. I told my niece, Jasmine, that I was getting ready emotionally for the day it really happened. She said, "Me, too." When I got to the car, I cried so hard I couldn't drive. Mama transitioned on July 6, 2019. Jasmine told me that when Nannie passed, she simply went to sleep peacefully. This would be the second time my niece witnessed death at that house. The first one was her grandfather ten years prior. She's so strong. She took care of Mama for about five years. Thank you, Jasmine. Now it's time for you to fly!

I Love Pink

We had the biggest party after the service. We ate, danced, and had a balloon release. Cousins and friends gathered to celebrate my mama, Aunt Annie Mae, Nannie, and friend.

We have begun to clean up and empty out her home. None of the family wants to live there, so we'll sell it. I have fond memories in the house. I found a straightening comb the other day, the one she used over thirty-four years ago to straighten my hair on my wedding day. I had gone out the night before and my hair had sweated out. She told me that there was no way I was going to get married with nappy hair. It was about three or four in the morning. My hair was fierce, but I had a few ear burns. It was so worth it. She was right—I was a beautiful bride.

She was more than a mom. She was my loving friend, cheerleader, counselor, finance officer, and spiritual advisor. I miss my mom and I know I will always.

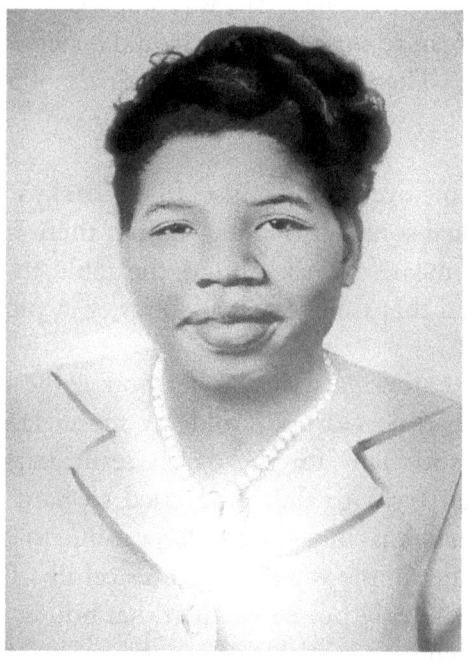

The Blank Page

The dead in Christ will rise first. — I THES 4:16

What comes to mind when you think about dying or losing someone you love?

_____

_____

_____

_____

_____

_____

_____

_____

_____

_____

_____

_____

_____

_____

Ouch
2011

OUCH! is a verbal response to a physical hurt. We use this word after a message from the nerve for pain has been sent. When a new mother of a young child asks her child, "Where does it hurt?" and the child responds, "All over," the mother knows that the pain is very deep.

OUCH! This pain is too much for me to bear.

OUCH, GOD! Can you remove this pain? I'm not Jesus!

OUCH! I know that you love me.

OUCH! Can you help me?

OUCH! You said you'll never leave me.

OUCH! Why don't you do something?

OUCH! Why, God? This pain is so different from the last pain.

OUCH! What about the pain that's so deep, you can't speak? God will heal even that.

OUCH! Now I understand.

OUCH! If I just shut up and stop complaining about where I am, I will grow out of this pain. This pain was not just for me. Others are watching my reaction to my OUCH!!!

The Other Side of 50
1-6-12

What's on the other side of 50?
EVERYTHING!
Grand events . . . Grand occasions
Grand parties and grandchildren
to live through and see yourself.
The other side of 50 is the time to enjoy
God's Great Earth:
Birds in flight, flowers, sunrises and
Golden orange sunsets
A time to embrace the hues of the changing seasons with their
beautiful display of colors
yellow, gold, auburn, and white.
What's on the other side of 50? SHOES!!!
Yellow, gold, auburn, white, and sometimes pink
A perfect size 6 1/2
When the enemy came in like a flood
God raised you up through his perfect love
and now that love overwhelms you like a blanket.
Being alone is pleasure.
You're confident that you are really never alone.
You have an understanding of whose you are
and make no excuses for who you are.
God's promises are manifested in your life
and in the lives of those you love
And those you have loved. Forgiveness is your blood.
You stood on faith and God has now placed you
on a national platform of grace.
On the other side of 50 is what you create.
You kept it real and now
He makes all things new!!!

My Reflections
Aging

Growing old is inevitable. The longer we live, the older we're going to get. Our bodies will start to reflect the aging process: Thinning hair, loss of sight and hearing. Our knees and other body parts will age. I turned sixty in September of 2019 and most days I feel great, but there are some days I have to push myself to move. My bones sound like popcorn when I walk. One thing I've learned is to remain positive about what is happening to my body, to stay physically active and think positive.

> "Finally, brothers and sisters, whatever is true, whatever is noble, whatever is right, whatever is pure, whatever is lovely, whatever is admirable—if anything is excellent or praiseworthy—think about such things" (Philippians 4:8).

I was inspired by my pastor to write this poem. I was praying for her one day at work and just began to write. I thought about her great courage over the years—how she stood strong in the face of calamity. Her grace under pressure was a lesson for me. This petite woman kept quiet to protect the church, herself, and her children from any negative repercussions from someone else's behavior and choices. She is my shero. She's a giant in the spirit. Her fiftieth birthday is a monument to the lives she has touched. I was so moved that when it was time for her birthday celebration, I asked if I could read this poem. I wrote it on January 6, and I think we had the gala celebration on January 14. I only had days to perfect this verbal tribute. It was going to be a relief for me to get this out of my heart and mind and through my mouth. The funny thing was that I never received a confirmation call, email, or text. God was still working, so I never really prepared to deliver this poem. I may have read it once. I knew what was in my heart. I just needed to get it out, not just for me, but for my pastor and for others. God just chose to sound the alarm in me in a different way—through this emotion of surprise.

I heard, "And now we will have Minister Dunk recite a poem." When my name was called, I froze. My husband said, "Whatcha gonna do?" I said, "I thought it was forgotten. I left my papers in the car!" I was thinking, would I dare to run to the car and make everyone wait on me? No! I had to think quickly. I found the poem in my phone and read it. It was a different version. Everyone knew me as "the church clown," so they knew I was going to be funny. I don't plan to be funny; it just happens.

I did not disappoint. My entrance was funny and not as graceful as I would have liked it to be. As I started walking up the stairs, my long skirt got caught and I nearly fell. When I got to the mic, I got my skirt together and took a deep breath. I told the audience to be careful what you ask God for. I had such a fun, goofy time reading that poem.

After I finished, I looked at my pastor. She was laughing, which put me at ease. I was both surprised and humbled. I learned that we must be ready when God says yes. Stand with grace and humility. Thank God for technology and a merry heart!

The Blank Page

They will still bear fruit in old age, they will stay fresh and green. —PS 92:14

How do you feel about aging?.

_____

_____

_____

_____

_____

_____

_____

_____

_____

_____

_____

_____

_____

SECTION XII

Boldness

Be Bold

Are you ready to be bold?
What does your future hold?
Will you be cold or will you unfold
Like an ocean to behold
What were you told as you grew old?
What will you say as your story unfolds
Will it be like mold, exposed and uncontrolled
Or will it be closed?
Will it contain platinum or gold?
Declare it, don't withhold it
Or you may be scolded and opposed
Decide to disclose your truth
You must be sold on your destiny
Be black, be beautiful
Be bold

I Love Pink

Living Our Dreams
1-9-12

Living our dream is
more than a white picket fence,
a Benz, a pool, or some fairytale lie.
Living our dream is real and tangible.
We have made sacrifices for the future
right in the middle of our present
learning from the past.
We have defied the repetition . . . the repetition . . .
the repetition . . .
that keeps a people chained
to the mistakes of the past.
King had a dream
but had to live a different reality
and he was colored.
Obama lived the dream that King had
and created a unique opportunity
to become president
and he was colored!
Don't you have a dream?
I have a dream
that one day I will become a millionaire!
Where's my reality
my white picket fence, Benz, and pool?
Am I not living the dream of my ancestors?
who stood strong long ago
so that I might have the right to live
in a community of people from diverse backgrounds?
To thrive in an environment
where children can learn and grow
in school together.
A society that is not bound by skin color

I Love Pink

(like the past)
but by the content of our character.
OUR dream is a HOPE for something better than what we learned
from the past.
You may have a white picket fence,
a Benz, and a pool.
But please understand that those things only came with a price
Generations before went through
Great personal sacrifices, blood, sweat, and tears, through prayer,
praise, and worship.
I say to you today in our present,
LIVE THE DREAM!!! LIVE THE DREAM!!!
And BE THE DREAM!!

My Reflections
Boldness

While writing these poems, I was really feeling great as a woman of color. I was thinking about black history and what black people endured during the Civil Rights Era: the abuse, torture, and murder of innocent people for the color of their skin. I was thinking about the diverse community I live in. I'm thankful that the way was paved for my family to live in this neighborhood. Black and white people endured countless pressures from angry, fearful whites. Homes were burned down or bombed, and many people were beaten and lynched in the South. In her famous song, Billie Holiday called the lynchings "Strange Fruit." The words were written by a Jewish poet named Abel Meeropol.

> "Southern trees bearing strange fruit
> Blood on the leaves and blood at the roots
> Black bodies swinging in the southern breeze
> strange fruit hanging from the poplar trees."

Today, there's still strange fruit. Blacks are being mistreated and murdered by a vast majority of white police officers. I believe it goes back to how people are raised and what is spoken around them. Words have the power to heal or kill. My brother was shot by a police officer over thirty years ago. The officer had shot two others in a span of three weeks, one person before my brother and one person after my brother. After he shot the last person, the officer said he felt threatened because that person was holding a table knife.

In my brother's case, the officer said my brother attacked him after refusing to get out of the car. My brother had a mental disorder. He was schizophrenic and was off his meds. Why would this officer respond to a sensitive call like this one? It was bad judgment on his part and by his department. Families were affected by the mental state of this one police officer. Was it fear? Was there some other emotion driving him? We found out that he kept notches on his belt for the kills he had done like he was at the O.K. Corral. I have respect for police officers. I understand that it takes a different, mentally well-balanced person to fulfill that role in our communities. But this officer had a different mindset.

We chose to live in the community we live in; there were no restrictions. We were never beaten or harassed. My children went to school with whites, Hispanics, and other ethnic groups. Our neighbors are friendly and hardworking people of different races. One of our neighbors recently passed and he died alone, without any family. He was white, very friendly, and loved to talk to my husband. He had to call upon another neighbor, who's black, to be the executor of his estate. My, how times have changed! At his gravesite were ten people, all black except one. Again, my, how things have changed!

I was kind of feeling like a poet while writing this poem—Nikki Giovanni or Maya Angelou. My attitude was strong and bold. I really wanted to make a statement about how we can affect our future. I wanted to proclaim victory. We have learned from our past. We watched our ancestors press on in spite of the resistance. Our responsibility is not only to ourselves, but to our future generations. We can be bold and intentional with achieving more than the generations before us. We have to continue to dream and speak to anyone who dares to listen.

This cancer journey made me a stronger person who is in touch with all of who I am. I had to look cancer in the face and say, "God got it! Back up!" I'm not perfect, but I'm not the person I used to be, even before I started writing and rewriting this book. I never thought cancer could unfold my life in such an extraordinary way. I can look back over everything and truly say I've had a wonderful life.

I Have a Wonderful Life

I've learned to be smart,
courageous,
spirit-filled,
God-loving,
prayerful,
fearless,
loving,
kind,
emotionally balanced,
humble,
full of joy,
happy
a good listener,
attentive,
wise,
strong,
and bold!
And I'm more than a conqueror!

The Last Blank Page

What conclusions have you reached?

What are your personal takeaways?

Wrap Up

Thank you for taking this journey with me. My prayer is that God revealed something through the words that were written and the words you wrote, listed, or doodled. Cancer was the catalyst God used for me to recognize how I was emotionally paralyzed. I was stuck in bondage, not really knowing who I was—dead and numb to life. My life has been enriched through writing this book. I have dealt with many issues in my life and learned that healing is my portion. I learned that one emotion could just be a mask for other emotions needing to be dealt with.

My gifts and talents just laid dormant until the cancer. I'm still a work in progress. I still have to manage my emotions. Some days I have to put myself in time-out, some days I have to be quiet, and some days I speak loudly. Most days I'm living life to the fullest, with my emotions balanced.

Emotions are a part of us all. Our emotions need balance, and if they're not addressed, it can lead to deeper issues that will cause death, possible institutionalization, and reliance on prescription medications. I began this journey, as I wrote earlier, as a selfish endeavor. I discovered myself through writing and being connected to God. I had to come out of denial and develop a positive attitude about myself and my real life. I had to acknowledge my emotions, process and understand them, get to the root of them, and diminish any long-lasting effects I'd allowed my emotions to have by using the word of God. And I had to spend quality time with God.

God has continued to reveal himself to me. I can never be too busy to spend time with him. Spending quiet time with God helps me respond to situations rather than react. I realized I can spend time with God through dance, through being creative, or just through being intentional. When I'm prepping to minister, I often like to get quiet and be still. I want God to minister through me without any distractions.

I often tell my children to be quick to listen and slow to speak. I have peace. I know that I'm loved and I love myself. I trust God more and more. I have spoken these words on several occasions, at birthday celebrations, funerals, cancer awareness events, and even with my family. I'm often amazed at the reaction. I recited "Thank You, Cancer" last year at a cancer awareness event. They applauded. A few people came up to me and said they enjoyed the poem.

Words have the power to evoke feelings and emotions and to heal. Remember, if God has given you an assignment to write a book or start a business, please begin. He will provide what you need and give you the details. Trust the process. Rise up against the spirit of fear and begin your journey.

Please revisit the pages of my book in a few months and God will give you a fresh revelation. Once again, thank you for coming with me on my journey. Now begin yours.

Be Blessed, Be Beautiful, and Believe!

I Love Pink

Phyllis Dunk

Phyllis Dunk is not just a twenty-five-year breast cancer survivor and a nineteen-year colon cancer survivor. She's an ordained minister and playwright. She's been married for thirty-three years to her best friend and they have three grown children: a singer, a dancer, and an actor.

She believes God allowed cancer to be the catalyst to deliver her from herself emotionally and heal her physically. She began her journey through self-expression—journaling and writing poems. As she wrote, she realized she was processing emotions hidden deep inside. She knows God used the arts to stimulate her spiritual and emotional growth, molding her into freedom as a clown, actor, mime, director, dancer, and writer. She has been an associate minister for twenty-one years at Destiny Pointe Christian Center under the leadership of Pastor Renee Hornbuckle and has served there for twenty-eight years.

As a lifelong learner and creative, Phyllis can always be found on the internet, looking up how-tos, interesting words, or current or historical events, or working on a project, which she calls her therapy. Her latest creation is a memorial Mother's Day heart made out of costume jewelry her mother collected over the years.

She believes that words have the power to heal or kill, and it took her twenty-five years to release this powerful and revealing chronicle.

I Love Pink

www.ingramcontent.com/pod-product-compliance
Lightning Source LLC
Chambersburg PA
CBHW062221080426
42734CB00010B/1980